WILLIAM S. WIHR
Berkeley

WILLIAM S. WIHR
Berkeley

Survival Arts of
the Primitive Paiutes

MARGARET M. WHEAT

Survival Arts of the

Primitive Paiutes

University of Nevada Press · Reno, Nevada · 1967

University of Nevada Press
Reno, Nevada
© 1967 by University of Nevada Press
Library of Congress Catalog Card Number: 67–30392
Manufactured in the United States of America

For my husband, Wendell,
my first and best teacher
in wilderness survival.

Acknowledgments

While working on a study of the Pleistocene and Recent geology of the Great Basin during the late 1940's, I became interested in a related field—the antiquity of man in Western Nevada and the survival techniques of the people who had roamed the shores of now-extinct lakes. Until then very little had been recorded on the subject. At that time there was no trained resident anthropologist in Nevada. But in the meanwhile, the number of Old Indian People who personally knew the Old Ways was becoming smaller and smaller. So, in 1949, with a wire recorder loaned to me by Dr. Roger B. Morrison, and with cameras and expense money made available by the Nevada State Museum, I began recording and photographing the Northern Paiute Indians, hoping that those more knowledgeable than I might be able to interpret what I heard and saw.

I wish to thank the score or more of Indians who, without pay, gave many patient hours telling and retelling, demonstrating and explaining. They wanted a record of the Old Ways to be preserved for their own descendants and for the white man. To Wuzzie and Jimmy George, Edna and Willie Jones, Nina and Johnny Dunn, to Lily Shaw, Mabel Wright, Katy Frazier, Levi Frazier, Jr., Dora John, Harry Winnemucca, Alice Vidovich, and to Alice Steve—who reenacted those arts, some of which they still use and others which they had scarcely thought about for over half a century—I am completely indebted. To Andy Vidovich, Frank and Mamie John, Ethel and Herbert Pancho, to Eva Brown, Nellie Harnar, Nina Winnemucca and many more who, in song and story, were heard but are not seen here, I also wish to express my appreciation.

Without the aid and encouragement of many other friends through the years, I would have given up long ago. Dr. Gordon L. Grosscup gave more inspiration and material aid than he will ever know. Others in the field of anthropology—Donald R. Tuohy, Dr. Richard Shutler, Jr., Dr. Ethel E. Ewing, Dr. Charles Rozaire, Dr. Fritz Kramer, and many, many more—were kind and helpful beyond measure. Dr. Sven Liljeblad assisted unstintingly with the problem of linguistics. Thomas J. Trelease and others in the Nevada Fish and Game Commission, Dr. Richard G. Miller of Foresta Institute, David Marshall of the U.S. Fish and Wildlife Service, and Drs. Donald G. Cooney and

Ira La Rivers of the University of Nevada biology department graciously answered my numerous questions about fish, birds, plants, animals, and reptiles. Donald Bowers, Barbara Mauseth, and Beth Crittenden read and reread. Maya Miller, Barbara Silberling, Jean Hurd, Josette Gourley, and my cousin, Ruth Coleman, typed and took notes for many hours.

I wish to thank the Nevada State Museum, the board and its chairman, Judge Clark J. Guild, and the director, James Calhoun, not only for their initial help but also for permission to use the material gathered while they were assisting the project.

Dr. Omer C. Stewart's work, *Culture Element Distributions: Northern Paiutes,* was invaluable to me in tracking down the families in which the survival arts might be preserved. It is sad that we both could not have started a hundred years earlier.

May I also thank all of the children in the classrooms, and the adults in the social and service clubs to whom I talked, for their many challenging questions which sent me back to the Indians in search for answers.

Except for the old photos in Part II which were taken by a friend of my childhood, Mr. Roly Ham, I wish to take responsibility for the photography. It was difficult to choose from the nearly two thousand black-and-white and the many hundred color photos which were made for this study.

Last, but certainly not least, at the University of Nevada Press, I wish to thank Robert Laxalt, Yolande Sheppard, and Nicholas Cady for the delightful experience of working with them; and at home my gratitude goes to my own patient family: my children, Bill, Jack, Sylvia, and Don Hatton, and Jerry Wheat and my husband, Wendell.

Carson City, Nevada   M.M.W.
Summer, 1967

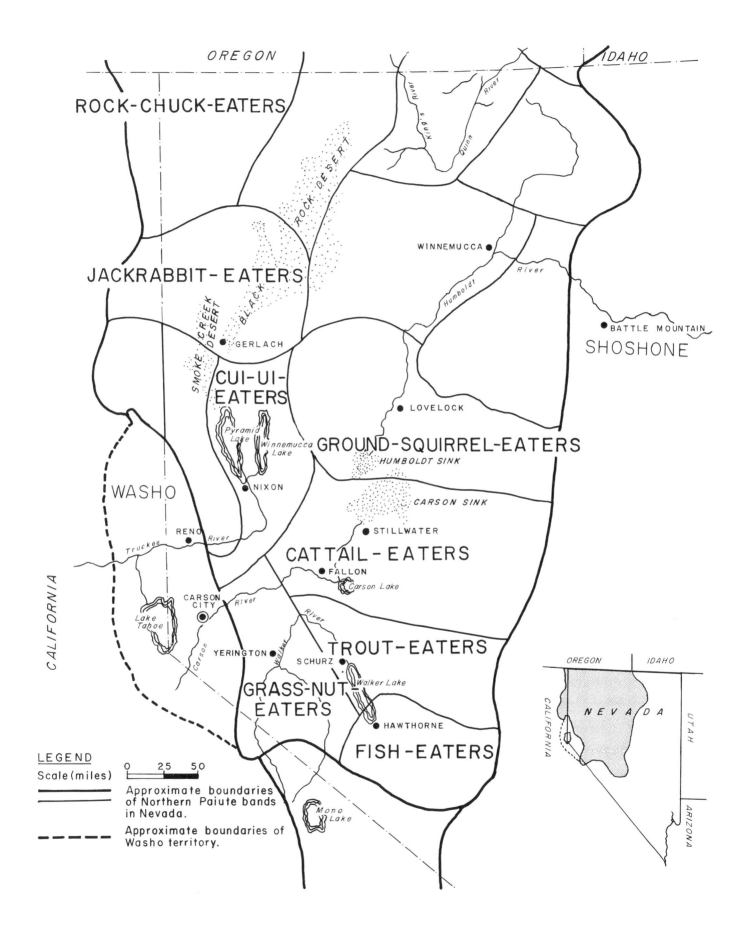

ROCK-CHUCK-EATERS

OREGON

IDAHO

JACKRABBIT-EATERS

ROCK DESERT

King's River

Quinn River

WINNEMUCCA

Humboldt River

BATTLE MOUNTAIN

SHOSHONE

SMOKE CREEK DESERT

BLACK

GERLACH

CUI-UI-EATERS

Pyramid Lake

Winnemucca Lake

LOVELOCK

GROUND-SQUIRREL-EATERS

HUMBOLDT SINK

WASHO

NIXON

CARSON SINK

RENO

Truckee River

STILLWATER

CATTAIL-EATERS

FALLON

Carson Lake

CALIFORNIA

Lake Tahoe

CARSON CITY

Carson River

River

YERINGTON

Walker

SCHURZ

TROUT-EATERS

GRASS-NUT-EATERS

Walker Lake

HAWTHORNE

FISH-EATERS

LEGEND

Scale (miles)

0   25   50

Approximate boundaries
of Northern Paiute bands
in Nevada.

Approximate boundaries of
Washo territory.

Mono Lake

OREGON   IDAHO

CALIFORNIA

NEVADA

UTAH

ARIZONA

Contents

Introduction

This is the story of the Indian people who were living in the western part of Nevada when the thin line of prospectors and pioneers crossed their land in 1849 enroute to the riches of California. It is the story of a people whose parents hunted with bows and arrows in a non-pottery culture and whose children watched the launching of a space probe on their TV sets; whose fathers had no government and whose sons voted for presidents. This is the story of a woman who harvested worms from pine trees for food and whose daughter studied bacteriology in college; of a man who painted his sons with the red earth-paints of the desert in order that the fast bullets of World War II would pass over their heads and the slow ones would fall short. This is the story of the way people survived using only tools made from the bone, sinew, and hides of animals, from the fibers and stems of plants, and from the stones of the desert.

The Old People
and the Land

I

The Old People
and the Land

THE GREAT BASIN

Before gold was discovered in California at Sutter's Mill in 1848, little was known of that vast area of the West now comprising the states of Nevada and Utah. Only a handful of white men had attempted to cross the forbidding expanse of desert that lies between the Sierra Nevada mountains of western Nevada and the Wasatch Mountains of central Utah—an area nearly as large as France.

In the decade between 1832 and 1843, small groups of trappers and explorers had risked their lives to find the beaver-filled rivers which the cartographers had drawn onto maps of the area. John C. Frémont,[1] with his exploration party of 1843, hoped to discover the Buenaventure,[2] a legendary river that was said to flow from the Rocky Mountains to the Pacific Ocean. If the river did indeed exist, he knew that it could provide the pathway across this unknown part of the West. Instead, he found only small, thirsty streams that vanished in dusty flatlands.

He named the region the Great Basin, a term leading many to envisage a vast, smooth bowl with a drain at the bottom, like a sink. A more accurate name would have been the Many Basins Province.

Here, over millions of years, huge blocks of land a dozen or more miles across be-

came tilted, their upturned edges forming the crest of one mountain range after another, each having one steep slope and one gentle slope. Between the ranges lay chains of basins, half-a-day's-walk wide, from which there was no drainage. During the Pleistocene these basins became filled with water, making lakes that rose and fell in rhythm with the periods of glaciation. At times of highest water many of the lakes joined at the passes, forming one huge lake that covered more than nine thousand square miles. On it a boat could have sailed 250 miles north and south, or 180 miles east and west. Geologists have given the name Lake Lahontan to this prehistoric body of water.[3] Today only two lakes of the great Lahontan system have not gone dry within the memory of man—Pyramid Lake and Walker Lake. Both are briny, containing the concentrate of the once great mother lake. Salts and minerals, concentrated in the drying lake, built weirdly-shaped castles and caverns of coral-like tufa, while waves sculptured hollows in tufa-cemented gravel and cut caves in rocky headlands. These became the grottoes for fish and later, when dry, shelter for animals.

As the lake receded, man entered the region to walk the shore line. He hunted and fished, leaving broken spears and discarded tools to record his presence. As the water dropped below the mouths of the caves, he took refuge in them, building his campfires to keep himself warm, burying his dead out of the reach of animals, and cacheing his food in the dark corners.[4] Camels, bison, shrub-oxen, and horses were probably his game.

Following the slow retreat of the shore line down the mountain slopes, generation after generation of Indians developed new skills and abandoned old ones. By the time the valley bottoms were dry and the once magnificent inland sea was reduced to reed-choked marshes and briny, treeless lakes, the Indians had learned to weave water-tight baskets and had discarded the atlatl for the bow and arrow. Most importantly, they learned to survive in an inhospitable land where short, green springs were followed by long, brown summers and clear, cold winters.

The country inhabited by these Indians lay in the rain-shadow east of the Sierra Nevada mountains. Wet storms rolling in off the Pacific Ocean and across California were lifted up the western slope of the range. Here, tall, icy peaks drained the moisture from the wind as it passed. Pouring down the eastern slope of the mountains, the air, heated by compression, dried the rivers and streams, the ponds and lakes, the plants and animals, and the people. In summer the midday sun beat down on the clay and sand of the old lake floor, driving the rabbits, the lizards, and the coyotes into the uncertain shade of small, dry bushes. The setting sun took away the warmth, and in a moment the desert was chilled. Often the temperature dropped fifty degrees between noon and night. Winters were cold but dry. Snow that lasted more than a few days was rare in the valleys, but southern slopes, protected from the wind, warmed quickly in the midwinter sun. Then Indians and desert creatures alike came out of their shelters to hunt for food, hurrying back as the sun went down.

Rivers meander across the desert valleys,
cutting deep into old Lahontan lake beds. Here the sagebrush grow the tallest,
and the rabbits the fattest.

At the bottom of each valley was a lake or a marsh, depending on the water supply. The dwindling rivers which fed them wandered down the valleys, cutting deep into the old lake-bottom sands and silts. Along the banks the sagebrush grew twice as high and the cottontails twice as fat. Here there were trees—willows and cottonwoods—providing the only protection from the sun which the Indians did not make themselves.

In the Great Basin the marshes and playas were intermittent affairs, always at the mercy of dry cycles and shifting dunes and channels. In a half dozen years a marsh could change into a dust bowl, or conversely, a desert flat would be transformed into a luxuriant nesting ground for migratory water birds. Seeded by the wind the margins of the marshes became tangles of cattails and tules[5] that furnished roots for muskrats and man, grew leaves for the houses of blackbirds and man, and produced seeds for ducks and man.

Born in a few hours from flash floods were playa lakes. Thin sheets of water, miles across and ankle-deep, they might last a day, a week, or a month, but never long enough to support life. When the water was gone, the desert again became a white, glaring plane of hard-baked clay broken into myriads of hexagonal sections, and the Indians walked across rather than around it.

Two paces from the marsh's edge the desert began. Small grey-green sage and greasewood bushes covered the valley floors and carpeted the hill slopes. This was the home of the jackrabbit, the antelope, the wolf, and his tricky brother, the coyote. Here grew the tiny seeds that furnished much food for the Indians. Here also were the ground squirrels, rats, and birds which competed with the Indians for the seeds. Here were the cottontails, crickets, and caterpillars that ate the plants before the seeds matured. Here also went the Indians to harvest the rodents, the insects, and the birds.

Higher on the slopes where the weather

Great Basin Indians harvested much of their foodstuff from the dry, desert valleys.

was cooler and rainfall more frequent, junipers and nut-bearing piñon pines formed a thin mantle over the mountain tops. This was the home of the sagegrouse, the marmot, the deer, and the pika, or little-chief-rabbit, who made hay for his winter use. A few streams, which one could step across, traced their way among the pines and down through the sagebrush to disappear into the gravel at the mouths of the canyons. This was the deer-hunting, nut-gathering land of the Indians. If the nut crop failed, both the deer and the Indians grew lean.

Springs were remarkably common in the Great Basin, furnishing water for those who knew where and how to find it. In nearly every valley hot springs bubbled out along the fault line of the mountains' up-tilting, while clear, cold springs could be found in most of the ranges. Even so, no Indian ventured far without his water jug.

Bleak and cold, or hot and dry though the Great Basin was, the Indians found a livelihood there because they were wise in its ways and used every resource advantageously. Many adventurers who entered this barren country during the latter part of the nineteenth century died from heat and thirst in the summer, or from cold in the winter, or starved when they had exhausted the supplies they carried with them. Yet the Indians of the Great Basin were considered by the first explorers to be miserable creatures—even though they managed to survive where the white man could not.

They learned to build shelters from whatever material was available, protecting themselves in their seasonal wanderings from the extremes of the climate. They recognized and used small bits of food such as rodents, insects, roots, and tiny seeds which were rejected by the starving pioneers. They raised children and grew to old age. At times they even danced and sang.

Juniper and nut-bearing piñon pines scattered on the mountainsides overlooking a desert valley.

TROUT-EATERS, CUI-UI-EATERS, AND CATTAIL-EATERS

When the white man arrived in the Great Basin, he found five tribes of Indians locked off from the rest of the world by the high, snowcapped mountains on the west and the waterless deserts on the east. Four of the tribes belonged to one basic linguistic family, and the fifth spoke an alien tongue. In the southeast lived the Southern Paiutes, to the east were the Goshutes and the Shoshones, and in the northwest were the Northern Paiutes. The small unrelated group, the Washos, centered near Lake Tahoe.

Although the Northern Paiutes did not actually live in the Sierra Nevada, that towering range molded the pattern of their daily lives. It controlled the storms in the winter and captured the rainfall in the summer. It sent them fish-filled rivers to recharge their shrinking lakes and marshes, and it acted as a barrier to commerce with the rest of the world. And although the Indians were unaware of it, the Sierra Nevada possessed a treasure of gold which had been washed out of the rocks and held in pockets in the ancient riverbeds for some ninety million years. This treasure house was later to change the life of every Indian in the Basin when in one short decade thousands upon thousands of prospectors—good and bad, kind and cruel, wise and foolish—began to pour down the Humboldt River trail and across their land to the Mother Lode in California in 1849.

Before the land and its resources became the property of white men by arbitrary right of claim, the Indians freely roamed the Great Basin in a seasonal cycle to glean their subsistence. The quest for food was so pressing that many bands in the Great Basin became known for the food they most commonly used—the Ground-squirrel-eaters (kɨbídɨkaʔa), the Jackrabbit-eaters (kammídɨkaʔa), and the Sucker-eaters (pakwídɨkaʔa).

This is the story of the Trout-eaters (agáidɨkaʔa), the Cui-ui-eaters (kuyúidɨkaʔa), and the Cattail-eaters (tóidɨkaʔa) who lived in the western part of what is now Nevada. They were only three bands among twenty-three or more comprising the Northern Paiutes of Nevada, California, Idaho, and Oregon.

The Trout-eaters took their name from the huge salmon-trout (agai), now known as the Lahontan cutthroat, that lived in Walker Lake and spawned in the Walker River. This unique trout was a legacy from ancient Lake Lahontan where it evolved many thousands of years ago. The Trout-eaters made their headquarters at the mouth of the river, near their main source of food, but they also searched the desert and hills for seeds, roots, and nuts at ripening times.

The Cui-ui-eaters who lived on the shores of Pyramid Lake—seventy-five miles to the north—were named after a very different fish which white people later called the cui-ui. It was a large black fish of the sucker family, known only in Pyramid and Winnemucca lakes, a vestige of the vanished Lake Lahontan. Early in May, when the days began to grow warm, thousands of the big, ugly fish came from somewhere on the lake bottom to spawn in the Truckee River, after which they returned to the deep waters of the lake and were not seen until the following year. When Frémont and his exploring party visited the Cui-ui-eaters at the mouth of the Truckee River in January,

1844, he noted: "These Indians are very fat and appear to live an easy and happy life."[6]

The Cattail-eaters lived fifty miles to the east of Pyramid Lake in marshy areas near the sinks of the Carson and Humboldt rivers. Here, thousands of acres of land were covered with cattails and tules, rushes and nutgrass, making an ideal resting place for migratory water birds on the great flyway from Mexico to Canada. The roots and seeds of the marsh plants, the ducks and geese, and the little fish of the sloughs, along with the pinenuts from the mountains, formed the major foodstuffs for the Cattail-eaters. The pattern of life for these three bands was, for the most part, the pattern for all of the Northern Paiute Indians. Differences occurred where natural resources differed.

Agriculture was unknown to these groups in the northern part of the Great Basin where killing frosts came late in the spring and early in the fall. With a rainfall of only four to six inches per year, such crops as corn, beans, squash, and cotton could not be grown without irrigation.

Everywhere in the Basin the constant search went on from valley to lake, to mountain, to river, to marsh for water, food, and firewood, and for the materials out of which shelter and clothing and tools could be made.

Even in winter, when snow and cold hampered the ceaseless wanderings, camps were not permanent. Small family groups, made up of the head man and his wife or wives (who were invariably sisters), the children, a grandparent or two, and possibly an uncle, erected shelters near their caches of food. They chose locations which were protected from storms, where the creeks or springs remained open throughout the winter, and where firewood was available.

Without such tools as axe or saw, the supply of fuel which could be carried in bundles on the backs of women, and logs which could be dragged by men, soon became exhausted. Rather than search in ever widening circles around the winter camps, it was often more practical to move the family with its few belongings and build new shelters near a fresh supply of wood.

In fact, acquiring sufficient fuel was such a problem that it was one of the first chores assigned to children, and gathering firewood became part of the ceremony for a young Indian girl when she became a woman. An industrious girl who gathered large piles of wood, the Paiutes believed, would not be a lazy wife. In a culture where obtaining fuel and food was woman's work, a lazy wife could mean a cold, hungry family.

Early trappers and explorers recorded that the Basin Indians went naked most of the time, wearing only tunics of rabbit skins in winter.[7] Deer, whose hides could be used for buckskin clothing, were scarce in the Great Basin.[8] Antelope were much more plentiful on the rolling flanks of the mountain ranges, but to hunt and kill them was a community project. Mountain sheep were numerous but wary. Since all hides were at a premium they were used principally for such things as pouches to carry paints and other treasured possessions. An Indian fully dressed in skins was rare in the Basin, even in winter.

The rabbitskin blanket was the essential item of clothing, and at night it was both blanket and bed. Worn like a cape, it was tied by cordage around the neck and hung below the thighs. When an Indian's legs became cold while traveling, he merely squatted down and let the folds of the blanket warm them. A fortunate, or industrious, Indian might wear leather moccasins; but without a tanning process to make buckskin

*...elicans feeding on fish at the mouth
...f the Truckee River where it empties into Pyramid Lake.
...he mountains in the background show scars
...om the shoreline of Lake Lahontan.*

*Tules and cattails in the marshes
of the Great Basin provided an abundance of fish, game,
green food and building materials.*

waterproof, the Great Basin Indians more often resorted to pacs made of sagebrush bark which could be manufactured on the spot. At times, skirts of grass or shredded sagebrush bark were added to the women's costumes, topped by a bowl-shaped hat. Babies clad only in a string of beads found warmth in their cradleboards or under their mothers' rabbitskin blankets. If the snow were deep, leggings of skins or bark were occasionally worn.

Shelters were constructed by the women as they were needed. In the mountains, sagebrush pulled up by the roots and pine boughs broken from the trees were piled in a circle as high as a man's shoulders. Into this enclosure large logs could be dragged for a fire. Giving protection from the wind, such shelters were remarkably warm. On a journey, shelters just large enough to accommodate one person were often constructed for warmth in the winter and shade in the summer. These consisted simply of sufficient brush to span the distance from one bush to another, and they were just high enough to crawl under.

Near the marsh's edge more substantial dwellings that looked like huge overturned baskets were built of cattail mats tied onto willow frames, with a smoke hole left at the top. Against the wind and sun were made tightly-woven willow fences and shed-like structures with all manner of brush piled on top but often without walls. When the sun moved, the Indian moved.

If a death occurred in a dwelling, both it and the dead person's possessions were burned to prevent the ghost from returning to claim its belongings or to annoy the living. Otherwise, these shelters were patched and reinforced and reoccupied many times in the yearly rounds of food gathering.

THE CYCLE OF THE YEAR

January and February were critical months for the Great Basin Indians. Snow in the mountains covered their caches of nuts; ice formed on the marshes, sealing the fish and the cattail roots from their reach; seeds had been blown from the plants and were lost in the sand; and the rodents were in hibernation. Coyote and man alike hunted the hungry jackrabbits while they in turn were searching for food.

In January occasional winter trout (tommó'agai) left the lake to spawn in the river. To catch them, groups of men working together built weirs of willow screens tied to cottonwood poles stuck in the river mud. In the center a platform was built where a man could sit wrapped in his rabbitskin blanket. Holding a net tied to an H- or A-shaped willow frame, the Indian scooped up the fish as they milled about against the weir below him. Many of the fish weighed more than ten pounds. Limiting himself to five fish, a sacred number with the Paiutes, each man in turn relinquished his place to a friend who warmed himself by a fire burning on the river bank.

About the middle of February the hunting improved somewhat when the ground squirrels (kɨbɨ) came out of hibernation. They were thin, but when roasted in hot coals they were welcome game to the hunter and his family. To catch them the men and the older boys closed all but one entrance to the burrows. Then, waiting patiently by the single opening until the squirrels ventured out, the men shot them with bows and arrows. These arrows were not always stone-tipped. Often they were simply greasewood or rosewood shafts with blunt ends which only stunned the animals until the hunter could kill them. By early summer these squirrels became so fat they could be caught by swift runners.

The roasting process was not wasteful. After the squirrels were singed in the hot coals and the scorched hair removed with a grass brush, they were opened and the entrails stripped of their contents before being tucked back and pinned into the body cavity. Tossed onto the coals, they were then roasted—head and all. Occasionally they were cooked as they came from the hunt, without cleaning or dressing. Children were especially fond of sticking their fingers into the warm juices inside the squirrels and licking them, as modern children lick cake-batter, and they liked to suck the brains from the skull, like marrow from a bone.

RETURN OF SPRING

As the days became warmer in March, great flocks of birds left their winter feeding grounds in lands far to the south and returned by the thousands to the marshes of the Great Basin. Blackening the sky with their formations and drowning all other sound with their squawking, they served notice that spring had arrived. There were snow geese that stopped to feed and Canada geese (nagíta) that often stayed to nest. There were ducks—mallards, pintails, canvasbacks, the goldeneye called "big-head," the shovelers called "big-nose," and the hen ducks (all the hens were thought to be of one breed, for "only the drakes are different"). There were the shore birds—the stilts and the avocets who were "the same birds in different clothes," the phala-

ropes, the curlews, and the killdeer that, the Indians said, could whip up a dust storm by flying in circles while crying their plaintive songs. And there were the great white pelicans that glided endlessly like strings of pearls high in the sky until it was time for nesting on the sand dune island in the Carson Sink and on Anahoe Island in Pyramid Lake. The Paiutes knew when to expect their return and listened for their first call.

Spring was a good time. It meant that the new shoots of the cattail would soon appear above the water. Impatient for fresh green food, naked women waded into the marshes, reaching arm-deep into the chilly water to search in the mud. The shoots were covered with soggy brown leaves that the mothers peeled off with their thumbnails before passing the white spears to the hungry children who sat huddled in their blankets on the banks.

When the desert began to show green, the Indians competed with rabbits for the small flat plants called carved-seed (kammísiki) that spread out on the adjacent sand hills, eating them raw as the jackrabbit did. Women and children scratched among the desert bushes for roots which could be boiled and eaten, and gathered the first leaves of the squaw cabbage, which had to be boiled twice to remove the bitterness.

The men made boat-like rafts of dry, pithy tules tied in bundles, which they maneuvered in and out of the clumps of reeds in search of eggs, not caring whether they were fresh or partially incubated. Women wove bag-like baskets of green tules to carry home eggs found on the shore. The baskets were quickly made and as casually discarded, like the modern shopping bag.

Netting ducks was a man's job. He hung his net at an angle above the water, supporting it on forked sticks thrust into the mud. When the feeding ducks swam toward the net, the hunter jumped from his hiding place in the tules. The ducks, when startled, would fly straight up with their necks extended and become entangled in the net, pulling it down upon themselves.

Like the squirrels, the ducks were roasted in the coals. Sometimes they were rolled in mud with the feathers left on and then buried in the coals. When they were taken out, the mud, feathers, and skin were peeled off leaving the meat juicy, tender, and clean.

Mudhens, more properly called coots, were often skinned before roasting. Their skins would be cut in long narrow strips, wound around cordage for additional strength, and woven into blankets. The skin from the breasts of swans, with its thick white down, was prized for the babies' pillows in cradleboards.

In May, thousands of shiners, suckers, cui-ui, and huge spring trout (tamá'agai) started their spawning run up the Truckee and Walker rivers. Paiutes from miles around flocked to the mouths of the rivers to join their "cousins," the Trout-eaters and the Cui-ui-eaters.[9] If famine had occurred during the winter, the weak ones often perished before reaching their destination—or failed to survive the feast.

The fish runs were influenced by the temperature and the amount of fresh water the rivers emptied into the brackish lakes. At times only a single fish or two could be seen. At other times they were so thick that men speared them by the hundreds, and children drove them into shallow water and, throwing themselves on the fish, caught them in their arms. Along the riverbank, fires were built of driftwood, and the huge cutthroat trout were laid whole on the hot coals. After they were baked the skin was peeled back exposing what explorers described as "the finest fish-flesh in the world." The Indians gorged themselves for days.

The women, eager for gossip after the long winter months, sat in groups while they cut each fish down the back with their stone knives. They laid the fish out to dry on bushes or across racks made of sticks, with "the meat side up and the fur side down." Overhead, black-wing-tipped pelicans circled majestically, while down on the delta, noisy gulls fought over the offal that floated down the river. When dry, the fish were stacked like firewood in the sun or hung by their tails from the willow frames of the houses. The cui-ui, so rich in oil, soon became rancid. The Indians were accustomed to this just as they were accustomed to the fishy flavor of the pelican eggs robbed from the nesting ground. "When you're hungry, you eat anything."

By the first of June the early desert seeds were ripe for gathering; the tiny mustard seed (atsá, which means red) was followed by the mentzelia seed (kuhá) that has a nutty flavor and is given to the old people when they are not feeling well. To gather the many varieties of small seeds, the women used finely-woven winnowing baskets onto which they beat the seeds from the plants.

Sometimes word would reach a family that the little red berry of the desert-thorn (húupui, or red-eye) was ripe and plentiful in a valley fifty miles away. Off the Indians would go to gather as many berries as they could before the ground squirrel ate them all. Every night the men set deadfalls to catch a few rats, squirrels, or birds to supplement the diet. When one crop was harvested they knew where the next one was ripening, and so over the hills they trudged again, with their baskets, blankets, water jugs, and their babies on their backs, sleeping wherever night found them.

This was the season when the young jack-rabbits were especially good to eat. They provided many a little Indian boy with his first kill, which he would proudly present to his old aunt or grandmother. After she had boiled the rabbit, she chewed the meat to a pulp and rubbed it on the young hunter—on his wrists, and inside his knees and elbows. The rest of the family could eat of his first game, but he could not.[10]

SUMMER HARVEST

Back in the marshes the ducklings were getting fat and noisy and the old ducks were molting their flight feathers. Men on their tule rafts drove the helpless ducks out of the water onto land, where, half running and half airborne, they tried to escape the swiftest of the Indian runners in a hockey-like chase. If more birds were caught than could be eaten immediately, they, like the fish, were split open and dried.

In July, the Indian rice grass (wái) was ready to harvest. Before the nutritious seeds fell to the ground, the women cut great arm-loads of the grass to be carried to threshing pads of sun-baked earth. Here, in the cool of the day, old women singed off the little black seeds which clung so stubbornly to the stems. Moistening the sheaves to retard flash burning, they placed handfuls on a small fire. As the grass was consumed, the hard-shelled seeds dropped, roasted, into the ash. Later they were cleaned on a winnowing basket and husked on a flat stone to make meal for gruel.[11]

In the marshes, the golden pollen-spikes of the cattail blazed in the sun. Baskets of pollen could be collected in a short time. It was then made into one of the few bread-like foods used by the Paiutes. Green cattail leaves were laid across a bed of hot coals. The pollen, mixed with a little water and formed into cakes, was put on the leaves. Then, a second layer of leaves and coals was placed over this to bake the tops of the cakes.

After the cattail pollen, buckberries matured about the first of August. The low buckberry trees were found in groves along many of the river bottoms, where they formed thorny thickets that covered thousands of acres. The small red berries dotting the olive green branches were tart and full of seeds, but were probably the most abundant berry in the Basin. The Indians assembled in the groves with their winnowing trays and their sticks to beat the berries from the trees. A sugarless sauce was made by hand-pressing the berries through a basketry sieve. The sieve looked like a miniature winnowing tray with small holes. Surplus berries were sun-dried for winter use.

Buckberry groves were pleasant places in the summer when it was hot. They were shady, lazy places where the robins, flickers, and crows also gathered to eat the berries, where magpies nested, and the cottontails were plentiful. The Indians ate the robins and caught the magpies to get the beautiful, magical, irridescent feathers from which the men made dance skirts and bonnets. Bobcats hunted the birds, and the Indians hunted the bobcats for their pelts, which were especially prized for making quivers.

At night the great horned owl (muhú) hooted her frightening cry in the low branches overhead. Indian mothers told their children that it was the voice of an old woman who was looking for children to eat. If the old woman heard a child crying, she would come to get it, carrying her basket on her back. The basket had a spike in the bottom, they said, and the old woman would throw the child over her shoulder into the basket and take him away. This was one of the reasons Paiute children seldom cried.

FALL AND PINENUT TIME

For the Indians in Nevada, pinenut time was the most important time of the year. Religion was combined with play, work with happiness. First, the best crop of nuts had to be located. Trees on one mountain range would be heavy with nuts one year, but the next year the yield might occur on a range fifty miles away. In August, scouts were sent to the mountains to find the most promising pinenut area. The scouts returned carrying a small pine bough on which hung a few immature cones, the sign of a good crop. Then, plans were made for the annual prayer-dance.

First, enough nuts had to be gathered for the occasion so that everyone received a few. The Paiutes believed that the ritual for gathering these nuts should be properly observed. So, before the sun was up, a small party of men and women left their camp in the valley for the pinenut forest, carrying harvesting baskets, water jugs, and a small supply of cattail seeds—the most nourishing food for a journey.

At the pinenut groves, they arose early and as the sun came up they prayed to the "People's Father" (nimínnaa) asking that they should "feel good and not be sick." Then they dug a pit, and in it built a fire large enough to heat the bottom and the rim of dirt around it. One Indian remained close to camp during the day to tend the fire, while the others collected a few baskets of immature cones which had not yet opened.

When the gatherers returned with their cones at midday, they removed the live coals from the pit, which by then was very hot. Dumping in the cones, they pushed the hot earth back over the nuts and built another fire on top. An old woman, who had been taken along because she had special powers, told the "ghosts" to go away because the Indians did not want harm to come to the nuts or the maturing crop. She picked up a handful of dirt and threw it "at the ghosts to the north, and another at the ghosts to the south, and then another to the east, chasing them that way."

After an hour or two of roasting, the green cones were opened and the nuts laboriously removed. Later in the season, after the cones had matured, the nuts could be gathered more easily.

When the party had collected enough nuts for everyone at camp, it returned from the hills carrying a small tree to "show what they were dancing for"—and the formal ceremony began.

A pinenut prayer-dance was an all-night affair starting when the sun went down. With shoulder touching shoulder, the Indians formed a tight circle around the tree. When the Man-Who-Knows-Many-Songs started to sing, the people began moving to the left with a slow, shuffling step. Some songs belonged to all of the Indians; others were the personal property of those who had received them in their dreams. If the owner sang his song, it was permissible for all to join him. The Paiute Indians believed that great power lay in songs and dancing, so this was one of their ways of praying. They believed that if they danced the pinenut dance, the rains would come and the nuts would not dry up.

As the dancing circle moved slowly clockwise, an old lady carrying a basket of water walked in the opposite direction around the outside of the dancers. Dipping a twig of sagebrush in the water, she sprinkled the ground as she prayed for rain and many nuts.[12] She had chosen the twig with reverence for it was believed the sagebrush, too, had the power to make rain. The twig was from the fresh new growth on the bush, usually bearing a plume of tiny green sage flowers.

Next she carried a small basket of pine-nuts around the circle, scattering them on the ground as she walked, because the Indian believed that whenever they took something from the earth they were obliged to give back something in return. If, for instance, they dug up a root, they returned a stick, a bead, or a stone. After the coming of the white man they often substituted small pieces of rag or pins as gifts to the earth. No one picked up these offerings because they had been given in payment and it would have been considered stealing to take them.

At midnight the old lady distributed a small number of nuts into the outstretched hands of the dancers, to be eaten while they rested. Then the dance resumed and the monotonous circling continued until the sun came up in the morning.

As the day grew warm, tired Indians slept, half shaded by sagebrush shelters too small to stand in. Naked children made little figures of clay or played in the dust and ashes. When the evening grew cool, bringing the mosquitoes (mopóŋɨ) out of the marshes, the Indians stirred from their resting places to build smoky fires to drive the insects away.

After eating whatever was available they assembled to play the highly complicated hand game. This was a gambling sport in which they often bet everything they owned —their blankets, baskets, and their beads. The games often lasted four or five days without stopping; as one game was finished the next one started. When players grew tired, they simply got up and moved a few feet away into the brush to sleep, letting others take their places.

Usually one family played against another family, or one band against another band. If one woman bet a basket, a woman from the other side matched it with a basket of equal value. A rabbitskin blanket was bet against another rabbitskin blanket, a string of beads against another string of beads. When all bets were in and balanced, a process that often took hours of dickering, the two sides sat on the ground facing each other. The hand game was also a singing game, and in front of each group was a log on which to beat out the rhythm of the songs with sticks. Ten tally sticks and the bets were heaped between the two sides.

To play the game, two people on one side each concealed a pair of sticks or "bones" within their closed fists. One bone of each pair was plain, the other ornamented. The guesser on the opposing team had to choose in which hands the unornamented sticks were hidden. If the guess were correct, his side was awarded a tally stick. If not, his side lost a stick. The side winning all ten tally sticks claimed all the bets. The singers opposing the guesser shouted, waved, and beat the logs to confuse him, but he sat quietly, apparently oblivious to the distractions, concentrating on his choice. It is remarkable how often a good guesser won. Winners were never congratulated, nor were losers ever consoled. This game is still played in the Great Basin with stakes often running into hundreds of dollars.

After the pinenut celebration was over, the Indians returned to their daily routine until the rose hips turned red in the valley. Then they knew that the pinenuts were ripe in the hills. This was the signal for them to put their possessions on their backs again and move on.

Pinenut time was a happy time for the Indian people. They loved the cool, crisp air of the hills after the shadeless desert. They emptied their willow jugs of the tepid, alkaline water of the marshes and refilled them from mountain springs, careful lest they break the waving banners of algae in the flowing water. "When moss is growing in water like long hair, you don't take it out," the Indians believed. "You leave it there. If you don't leave it there, the water will dry up because it is 'her' hair."

Cool water was considered to be a cure for all ailments, so they prayed to it, asking for good health and strength. The women built shelters of sage and pine boughs while the men hunted the mountain meadows for sagehens and squirrels, and the rocky slides for marmots. Children and old ones collected wood for the evening fires that dotted the range like beacons of friendship.

Starting at the lower foothills, they worked their way up the slopes as the nuts ripened during the fall months. Everyone worked—collecting, carrying, cleaning, roasting, and grinding. Cones which had not yet opened were stored in piles in shallow, grass-lined pits and covered with more grass, brush, and heavy stones. When they opened the caches in late spring, the cones would have burst, freeing the seeds. No attempt was made to conceal the piles, for looting never occurred. Everyone recognized his own hoard, and did not molest his neighbor's.[13]

BEFORE THE SNOW FLIES

In November, the rabbit-hunt captain sent word through the hills that a rabbit drive was to be held in the desert, so back went the strong and the swift to join in the hunt.

A rabbit drive was a community project. The rabbit-hunt captain chose the campsite for the first drive and built a big fire as a guide to the families moving down from the mountains. The firstcomers sang, played games, gambled, and courted while they waited for the others to assemble. Every prosperous family owned a rabbit net. These nets, made with two-inch mesh, were about three feet high. Their length depended on the owner's wishes, but they were often hundreds of feet long. The men strung the nets across the desert between bushes, or held them up with forked sticks stuck in the ground or with brush pulled out by the roots and piled in rows.

While the women stayed in camp gambling, the men—armed with sticks and bows and arrows—formed a moving fence, driving the rabbits ahead of them into the nets. Some hunters became famous as runners because they could overtake a jackrabbit on foot. Older men hid near the nets to remove and kill the rabbits as they became entangled in the mesh, and to set the nets up again.

At night the air was filled with the fragrance of sagebrush smoke and roasting meat and the sound of song and laughter. By the light of the campfire the men skinned the rabbits carefully and cut the pelts into long ribbons while they were still fresh and soft. The skinned rabbits which were not immediately eaten were dried and stored for the cold months ahead when they would be either boiled whole or pounded to a powder to make soup. The entire carcass was consumed—even the bones were ground and boiled.

Rabbit drives often became courting time for the Paiutes. There was no set pattern or firm rule for courtship. Usually the boy or his parents reached an understanding with the girl's parents, who had to confirm his ability as a hunter not only for the daughter's sake, but for their own security in old age.

To win a girl's favor, a boy brought her a duck or rabbit. If she rejected the gift, she rejected the boy. If a girl carried food or water to a boy she liked and the boy caught her wrist instead of accepting the gift, it meant he preferred the girl. As a girl reached marriageable age she often became the special charge of her grandmother, sleeping near her at night. There was no marriage ceremony. When a boy wanted to marry, he went to the girl's camp and sat all night near the place where she was sleeping. Each night he moved a little closer. If the girl wanted to reject her suitor, she moved her blanket near her mother's bed to sleep, and the boy abandoned his courtship.[14]

After the rabbit drive was over, many of the hunters went back to the hills where the little ones and the very old ones had been left—where thin, old hands had been gathering nuts from the ground as fast as hens pick up wheat in a chicken yard, and where the children had grown fat on the rich nutmeats.

APPROACH TO WINTER

When snow came, burying the fallen nuts that remained, many of the Cattail-eaters left the forest for their camps near the marshes, taking as much of the harvest as they could carry. There, the women built new houses or added new mats to their old ones. They wove tule mats for the floors where they slept and they gathered the seeds that had matured while they had been away in the hills. They beat the seablight seeds (wada) from the seablight bushes and cut armloads of long brown cattail heads which had seeds as fine as dust.

When needed in the winter, the women burst the cattail heads on the ground and sprinkled the fuzz with water in the same manner as they prepared the rice grass. Then, holding two sticks in each hand like tongs, they transferred the fuzz to the fire where it burned slowly, and the roasted seeds fell into the ashes. After the tiny seeds were cleaned of ash on a winnowing basket, they were made into a highly nutritious gruel.[15]

The seed heads of the nutgrass (áabi) had by this time opened like flowers. The seeds had fallen into the water and had been rafted against the marsh shore by the winds. The women strained out the seeds using fine-meshed winnowing baskets, and then carried them in tightly woven burden baskets to storage pits. Later, they could be ground without roasting, and boiled to make a gruel.

Ever busy, the women assembled their supplies of seeds, roots, pinenuts, and dried berries and put them into storage pits. They piled dried fish and rabbits on willow racks at the tops of their houses, hung jerky from roofs, and made small huts out of cattails to store willows for basket making, fiber for string making, and great hanks of rabbit-skin cordage for blankets.

After the first frost had killed the leaves, the men gathered bundles of hemp (wɨhá) from which they stripped the long, tough fibers to be stored in hanks until warm days, when they could sit in the sun and roll them into cordage between their naked thighs and their palms. Throughout the winter the men hunted everything that moved—except the coyote, the magpie, and the crow because they were carrion-eaters. They shot birds and rabbits with bows and arrows; they broke the ice with long, pointed rocks to catch small fish in the ponds; they trapped small rodents and birds between two flat rocks which were held apart by a delicate twig-and-string mechanism baited with pinenuts.

During the winter storms, the family huddled close to the small fire in the center of their snug shelter. The Old People rolled themselves up in their rabbitskin blankets and slept out the storm, stirring only when nature forced them to move.

In times of storm, usually only one meal a day was prepared. A small store of food was kept near the door, ready to be ground on the platter-shaped stone which lay on the floor. With a round stone held in her two hands, the mother or the grandmother pulverized small batches of nuts, seeds, and meat into a dark, coarse powder. Having no pottery, these Paiutes wove watertight baskets in which they made thick soup by adding water to the meal. To boil it, the cook lifted hot rocks from the fire and dropped them into the basket.[16]

Sitting around the cooking bowl, each member of the family dipped into the mixture, carrying it to his mouth with his index finger. At times the soup was dished into individual serving bowls which curiously resembled the women's hats in shape and construction. With his own bowl a person could ration himself at night, saving the remainder to be eaten cold—perhaps frozen—the next morning.

Wintertime was also the time for willow gathering and basket making. The women cut long, slender willow wands, now bare of leaves, and tied them into sheaves with willow withes. Those willows to be used for the weft were split into three parts; the pith and, later, the bark were peeled from the precious, white sapwood. The sapwood was smoothed to beautiful uniformity with flakes of stone and rolled into foot-wide hoops for storage. The long, straight willows were scraped of their bark, sorted for size, and tied into bundles for warp in making winnowing baskets, cradleboards, and all the baskets necessary for the Indians' way of life.

During the long winter evenings the family sat around the carefully tended fire listening to the wind rage against the thick matted walls. Children, warmly wrapped in their rabbitskin blankets, watched the shadows of woodpecker wings[17] flying like live birds in the updraft of the fire and said, "Grandfather, tell us a story." With the same tone of voice and the same motion of arms that he had learned from his grandfather, the old man recited the stories which could be told only in the winter months when the rattlesnake was in hibernation. Only the wind and the scrape-scrape of the women peeling willows broke the witchery of the story, a thousand times told.

As the pile of willow shavings grew higher in front of the weaver, the old grandfather would say to the little children, "Look! Look, see that willow-skin (sɨ̈bi puá). It was in such a pile of willow-skin that the Old Aunt hid the First Woman from her two sons, who were cannibals. . . ." And the story would go on and on, for a story once started had to be told to its conclusion even though drowsy little children fell asleep.

The Coming of the
White Man

II

The Coming of the
White Man

THE NEXT HUNDRED YEARS

In 1848, when the cry "Gold in California" rang through the nation, many thousands of people set out across rivers, plains, and mountains to seek their fortune. By the time they reached the land of the Paiutes they were tired and afraid; their animals were thin and footsore. Between the sink of the bitter, saline Humboldt River down which they had been traveling, and the fresh waters of the Carson and Truckee rivers ahead of them, lay forty miles of terrible desert where their wagon wheels would cut deep, dusty ruts in the fine sand and silt, and their oxen would lie down and die. Desperate in their struggle against heat and thirst, and fighting to push themselves and their possessions across this burning desert to safety, the forty-niners were seldom aware of the Indians who peered in wonder from behind sand hills and scattered greasewood at this endless human migration to some unknown land. The Indians waited patiently for this strange white tribe to pass, as the swans passed in the spring and fall. But the long line never ended.

Avoiding the path of the wagons and the white man's bewildering guns, the Indians went about the necessary business of gleaning food from the land. They crossed the trail of the white man at night, un-noticed, and went as usual to the rivers when the trout were running, or to the fields where the grass seeds were ripening, or to the mountains to gather pinenuts. They shared their food and hunting grounds with their "cousins" who had been pushed from their lands along the Humboldt River, now the highway of the emigrants.

With curiosity they inspected the abandoned wagons and frolicked among the bags of beans, throwing them in handfuls at each other; or believing that flour was the medicine paint of the white man (táiboʔo) they mixed it with water and smeared it on their rabbitskin blankets.[18] In later years they said ruefully, "We not know that stuff was grub." Occasionally they salvaged metal from the charred wagons to make crude cutting tools and arrow tips, or hung bits of discovered cloth around their waists for clothing. Otherwise their lives were little changed for ten years until, in 1859, silver was discovered in the Virginia Range, the mountains that separated the lands of the Washo and the Paiute.

With the opening of the mines on the Comstock, the horde of miners roared back over the Sierra. It was like a tidal wave that had gone out and was now rolling back to engulf the Indians. The cattlemen brought their herds to grow fat on the rice grass

This Indian house, probably constructed ca. 1900, was still in existence in the 1950's in Virginia City, Nevada.

seeds the Indians had formerly harvested every August. Woodcutters brought their axes and cut down the pinenut trees to feed the awful hunger of the furnaces in the stamp mills where ore was being ground to dust. Loggers and their oxen stripped the hill-home of the deer and sagehen for timbers to brace the mines which were boring ever deeper into the earth. The sheepherders turned their sheep onto the desert where the Indians hunted jackrabbits, and the sharp hooves cut down the delicate, edible desert plants. The miners spilled cyanide from their mills into the rivers and the fish died.

Some Indians retreated ever deeper into the unexplored back country, but the pros-

pectors followed them, seeking other ore bodies. Occasionally the Indians struck back by butchering stray cows and horses— so the white man's army came to protect the white man's property. Other Indians, hungry and bewildered, flocked to the mining camps to protest the cutting of the piñon trees—and were handed a sack of flour from the mills or a barrel of offal from the slaughterhouse. Women and children waited in line at the mouths of the mine tunnels when the men came off shift in the evening. The miners emptied the leftover bits of food from lunch pails into their outstretched baskets or poured cold coffee into their empty tin cans. In Virginia City, the Indians built houses of the same shape as the tule houses in the marshes, but now they used wire, boxes, boards, and sacks gathered from junk piles.

In May, 1860, all the Paiute bands, assembled for the cui-ui and trout runs at the mouth of the Truckee River, met in open conflict with a party of volunteer militia.[19] The dispute was over atrocities by both Indians and whites. When the battle was over, Pyramid Lake and part of the Truckee River were set aside as a reservation for the Cui-ui-eaters. Later, reservations were created for the Trout-eaters on Walker Lake, and land was allotted to the Cattail-eaters near the Carson Sink.

By 1870, new mines had been discovered

An Indian community near Stillwater, Nevada, before the turn of the century.

in central Nevada and the great freighting teams which supplied them were demanding more and more feed. In the land of the Cattail-eaters, the river bottoms and the edges of the marshes were fenced, and the wild grass was mowed for hay. The small town of Stillwater, Nevada, sprang up nearby and became the county seat of Churchill County. In 1873, Jim Richards built the first store there and gave the Indians their first white man's clothes—pants, shirts, and underwear for the men; yard goods, scarves, and underclothes for the women; combs and soap for all. For the first time the women covered the upper part of their bodies.

Soon irrigation was introduced and trees were planted around the new homes of the white men. Horses and cows were turned out into the desert to graze. Hogs, intended for sale at the mines, escaped from the ranches and went wild in the marshes, multiplying and growing fat on the tule roots, and devouring the broods of ducks and mudhens. As the hunting became poorer, the Indians established small rag-and-willow communities at the edges of the hay fields where the able men were hired to dig irrigation ditches and were taught to build fences. The young women began washing clothes and doing dishes in the homes of the white people while the old grandmothers and the old grandfathers cared for the little children and taught them the Old Ways.

By 1880, the trains were running across the reservations of the Cui-ui-eaters, and Captain Wasson had put his thumbprint on a right-of-way contract with the Carson & Colorado Railroad for the Trout-eaters. In return for the rights-of-way the Indians were given free passage anywhere on top of the box cars. So, many of them rode to the hop vineyards in California to earn money for horses and wagons.

The Indian Service opened a school at Stewart, Nevada, in 1890, and the Indian children were gathered in by persuasion and force to fill it. The girls were taught to sew and cook, to bake, and to can food. The boys learned to mend harnesses and to shoe horses, to use hammers, saws, and nails. They were all taught to read and write a little, and to count money—and were spanked if they spoke their own language. By intent or accident, the children became ashamed of the Old Ways and tried to forget them as soon as possible.

By the next generation many young people were more interested in the color of a dress or the breed of a horse than in the wrinkled old women who sat on the ground in the shade of a dirty canvas shelter, weaving their baskets and unraveling their memories.

THOSE WISE IN THE OLD WAYS

During the preparation of a geological report in 1949, it was necessary to find place-names for mountains that the white man had failed to christen. With pencil, paper, and wire recorder, I went to those Indians whom I had heard were wisest in the Old Ways.

Alice Steve, understanding the ways of both races, was the first.[20] Soon she brought her friend, Wuzzie George, and between them they poured out not only the names of the mountains and the valleys, but of the trees and the bushes that grew upon them and of the animals that lived in them. They told how and where the Old People had gathered seeds, roots, nuts, and berries. They took me to see the Doctor Rocks on which petroglyphs of people and circles had been made, they said, by Coyote.[21] We stopped to pray for a happy journey and left, in payment, a few pennies in the crannies with the buttons, safety pins, and beads already collected there. As we traveled, the two women pointed out the birds that were wicked, the birds that doctored the rattlesnakes, the birds that made the wind blow, and the birds that they ate. They told how the birds were caught and how they were cooked.

In this way I became an heir to the culture of many old Indians, assuming the role of the grandchild who, in the Old Days, listened and remembered. Forgetting the function of the wire recorder, they often reminded me to write down the stories they told. They sang the old songs and prayed the old prayers so that these would not be forgotten. For the camera, they demonstrated how they had helped the Old People build houses, how they gathered and ground seeds. Wuzzie's husband, Jimmy George, the last great shaman among the Paiutes in western Nevada, knew how to make rabbit-skin blankets, tule boats, and deadfalls. He could also make arrows and magpie-feather hats and deer-hoof rattles.[22]

The wire recorder was replaced by an early-model tape recorder which was heavy and clumsy and often difficult to carry to remote places. Despite that, the stock of tapes grew higher and higher.

Alice has since passed on to walk the Dusty Road with her ancestors, but her voice and wisdom remain. Wuzzie took me to her other friends—among them Edna Jones whose grandfather, Captain Wasson, was a leader among the Trout-eaters, and whose father (named Sing McMasters by

an Indian agent because he was the best singer) married both of Wasson's daughters.

When Edna was young, she went on many family rabbit drives with her numerous brothers and sisters because her grandfather had made one of the longest nets in the area. With great patience she instructed me in Indian etiquette, and because she had spent many years in school, she could translate Paiute thinking into the thinking of the white man. Edna's bead-and-leather work was among the finest. Edna's husband, Willie, made drums of rawhide and rattles from deer's ears with beads inside.[23]

One day Edna Jones took me to meet Nina Dunn, who made and beaded many of the beautiful cradleboards in use in Nevada today, and Johnny Dunn, who knew how to make string and spears and who tanned hides to cover Nina's cradleboards.

As time went by, the bulky tape recorder was replaced by a slim little instrument which rode on my back on our journeys afoot while the Indians showed the way. Mabel Wright, a Cui-ui-eater, cherished the Old Ways and the old songs. She told of the wonderful dream that had sustained her all her life. She sang of beautiful Pyramid Lake, that now was going dry because white people needed so much water elsewhere.[24]

So that her nieces and nephews could see a grass house like those the Old People lived in, she built one near the little town of Nixon, on Pyramid Lake. She had the frame nearly finished when she took me to see it, and I photographed it intermittently during the spring as the grass grew tall enough for her to weave the covering. Since then many others, charmed by a house constructed without boards or nails, have come to visit and photograph Mabel's house. When the hungry cows came down out of the hills, Mabel had to protect her house with a barbed-wire fence. During the winter of 1964, when the raging Truckee River was eating into the soft banks near Mabel's frame house, she gathered up her treasure and moved into the grass house on the sand hill. One day she wrapped herself in the rabbitskin blanket she had woven from the fur cordage made by her grandfather fifty years before. Then she sat for a picture on the sunny side of the grass house with her hair falling loose like the Old People's.

Katy Frazier was on her way to church in Nixon one Sunday morning when the cui-ui were running, but she consented to show how the fish were cut for drying. Laughingly she said she hoped she would not get blood on her church dress. Kneeling on the shores of Pyramid, she cut and cleaned the fish and washed them in the lake waters. After the photographs had been taken—and without a spot on her dress—she arrived at church before the last bell rang. Katy's eight children, thirty-one grandchildren, and fifteen great-grandchildren all like cui-ui, but few of them have ever eaten the fish dried, as the Old People did.

When he was quite young, Levi Frazier, Jr., learned to make arrowheads from Harry Winnemucca. By the time he was in high school he knew all the best places to gather obsidian. One day he cracked off a spall and completed a perfect point for me in four minutes.

WUZZIE GEORGE

Wuzzie George was, however, the acknowledged authority on the Old Ways. Everyone, even her husband, when at a loss for an answer, always replied, "You ask Wuzzie. Him know everything."

Most of Wuzzie's people were Cattail-eaters who had always lived by the marshes at the sink of the Carson River. However,

she explained that her grandfather's father was a Trout-eater who had walked to the land of the Cattail-eaters to join a rabbit drive long before anyone had seen a white man. During the days of dancing, he met a Cattail-eater girl and married her. He lived with her and her people until their two children were old enough to travel with him back to his own tribe on the shores of Walker Lake. His wife stayed behind with her people. In his own territory, he married again and when more babies began to arrive, his new wife wanted the Cattail-eater children returned to their mother. That is how Wuzzie happened to have cousins among the Trout-eaters.

One of these Cattail-eater children, Wuzzie's grandfather, was the man called Stovepipe by white people. Wuzzie claimed that Stovepipe was a good hunter because he made obsidian arrowheads and then pounded them fine and ate the chips. She wondered why it did not make him sick, but Stovepipe said that it made him feel good. Stovepipe married Mattie, who was almost grown before she saw a man with "white eyes" and much hair on his face. She had seen two of them riding south on horses and she had been terrified.

Describing the old life, Wuzzie tells a story that Mattie told her. "Before the [1860] war at Pyramid Lake, the Indians lived in tule houses for miles along the Carson Slough. Indians lived everyplace. Smoke all over when Indians build their fires in morning. That's what my grandmother said. When soldiers threw poison in river lots of them died. Killed lots of them. After that, not so many. My people in the mountains that time. That's what my grandma and grandpa always say. Stay over there on the mountains all winter, make house over there on mountain. That's why they never catch it, the poison. We call that place, where In-

Wuzzie gathering tules;
the white base of the stem,
which tastes quite bland,
was eaten raw.

Wuzzie gathering greasewood,
the fuel used by the Old People
for cooking and heating.

dians died, 'people's bones' (nɨmɨ́ʔohó)."[25]

Mattie and Stovepipe had five children, Wuzzie said, three boys and two girls. The oldest girl was called Mattie like her mother. She was much older than her sister Suzie, and when she grew up she married Sam Dick. Many years later, when Suzie was old enough to marry, she saw what a good provider Sam Dick was, and, following a custom among the Paiutes, she also became his wife. Wuzzie was the daughter of Suzie and Sam Dick.

By the time Wuzzie was born, about 1883, all the Cattail-eaters had moved out of the marshes and had attached themselves to the ranches at Stillwater, often adopting the names of the ranchers for whom they worked, and buying their clothes and flour at Jim Richards' store. Wuzzie was born one cold night in the mountains during pinenut time. The morning after her birth,

her father broke the ice at the spring and took a bath to show that he was not "lazy." He didn't sleep for ten days, Wuzzie recounted, but kept the fire burning. He didn't hunt for ten days, either. Then he left the first thing he killed where it was, as "a kind of payment."

Besides being a good hunter, according to Wuzzie, Sam Dick was a good worker. He earned bacon, flour, and some money when he worked for white people, so there was always food for his family, including Mattie and Stovepipe. From the white man he learned to build a small house, "a kind of cellar" of sticks and mud to keep ducks, geese, mudhens, wild pigs,[26] and horse meat from spoiling. But her grandmother preferred to bury the eggs in the cool, moist sand in the old fashioned pits.

MATTIE, WIFE OF STOVEPIPE

When Wuzzie was a little girl, her grandmother Mattie took care of her while her

22

*In early August
Wuzzie beats little red "buckberries"
into her winnowing tray.*

*The seeds of many desert plants
mature in late summer.
They are gathered and cleaned
on winnowing trays.*

mother washed dishes in the hotel at Stillwater. Every day old Mattie and Wuzzie went to the hard, salty flats where the biggest greasewood grew, to gather fuel for the kitchen stove in the hotel where Suzie worked. The hotel people gave them breakfast in exchange for the wood. Other Indians had to pay fifteen cents a meal when they ate at the hotel. While she was gathering the wood, Mattie always watched for the greasewood worms which lived in the roots of the plants. They were inch-long white grubs with dark heads. She dug them out of the roots with a stick, tied them up in a rag and took them home. After she had roasted them in hot coals she shared them with Wuzzie. Wuzzie remembered they tasted greasy. They could be found only in the summer because the cold weather drove them too deep into the ground.

Wuzzie and Mattie walked wherever they went because Mattie and Stovepipe never owned a horse and wagon. They walked to go fishing in the sloughs, to gather berries and dig roots in the river bottoms, to pull pale green tule stems and white cattail roots in the marshes, to collect pine pollen in the mountains and honeydew from the cane

*Cattail shoots are peeled and eaten raw,
while the rhizomes are baked in hot coals.*

that grew by the springs.[27] In summer when they visited friends far away they traveled mostly in the cool of the night, sleeping by the trail in the day.

After the leaves fell, they walked to the places where the willows grew straight and tall, and Mattie cut as many as she could carry home on her back in huge bundles. Wuzzie often sat with Mattie in the winter

23

A small "nut," which tastes much like coconut,
is attached by a long slender root
to a river-bottom grass commonly known as taboose.
In the fall, Indian women dug them
with pointed sticks which
had been hardened by fire.

Many kinds of pollen, including pine pollen,
were gathered in the spring.

These typical desert roots supplied
a large proportion of the Indian diet.

"Rabbit's lettuce" (carved seed) was one
of the first food plants available
in the spring; it was eaten raw.

Honeydew from this cane was the major sweet
of the Indians. The cane was also used
for arrow shafts.

The tiny black seeds from Indian rice-grass
was one of the main sources of food
for Great Basin Indians.

Indian women, ca. 1900, resting by the trail.

The white man's influence is shown
in the changing shape of woven water jugs.
The jug on the left is from pre-white days;
the one in the center is patterned after
the miners' "little brown jug"; the third copies
the U.S. Army canteen.

A cooking basket with a stirring stick,
and personal eating dish. The eating dish is
identical to the hat used by women to protect
their heads from the tumpline.

The end of this stirring stick
has been worn thin by long use.

sun behind an old canvas windbreak, talking of Old Things while sorting and preparing the willows for future use.

Mattie made willow water jugs, shaped like fat bottles, woven so fine that they scarcely leaked even without the coating of red clay and hot pitch which she smeared on the outside. Mattie and Wuzzie always carried jugs of this sort when they went into the desert. They were lightweight and unbreakable. Moisture seeping through the willow-work evaporated and kept the water cool for drinking. Wuzzie said that some jugs were big, holding five gallons or more.

The greatest skill of all, however, was needed in making the close-woven cooking

25

*Winnowing baskets were of great importance
for gathering and preparing food.
Size and weave depended on their use.
The large, coarse-woven trays, which were expendable,
were used for netting minnows, serving roasted
or boiled squirrel, duck, fish, and rabbit,
and for drying meat. They were patched
and mended until too worn to use again.
The fine-woven trays and the small beater
were used for gathering seeds.*

*A parching-tray with pine nuts,
and a sieve for separating seeds
from mashed berries.*

*Two metates with manos;
the huller on the larger metate has a flat bottom
for cracking shells and husks.*

*A coarse-woven conical burden basket;
fine-woven burden baskets were used
for carrying small seeds.*

baskets. Unlike water jugs, they could not
be coated with pitch because the heat
would melt the pitch. Since a basket would
burn if placed directly upon the fire, the
Paiutes dropped hot rocks into the liquid
to boil their food. Wuzzie never learned to
weave cooking baskets because Suzie, her
mother, used the heavy iron frying pans

*Wuzzie demonstrates typical kitchen tools
of the Old People.*

Wuzzie straining grit from her red paint.

Balls of dried red pigment are still in demand. Red paint is used for good luck, medicinal purposes, and decoration.

and dutch ovens that were available at Jim Richards' store. But she watched Mattie make cooking baskets and helped her bend and tie green willows into loops with handles for stirring sticks.

FOLLOWING MATTIE'S TRAIL

Following the trail she had walked with her grandmother many years before, Wuzzie led her friends and me to the place where Mattie had gathered the roots of the Indian potato and where, as a child, Wuzzie had nibbled on the peeled stems of the thistle. The Old Ladies always carried long walking sticks for ease in climbing the hills and to guard against snakes. They put red rags or red paint on their shoes because, they said, "Rattlesnakes don't like red."

Red paint was also considered to cure many ailments and to prevent many more. The Old People painted their faces for decoration, mothers put it on babies' chafed bottoms, and, because they believed it had a magic power, the Indians painted arrows, caves, and their own bodies with red paint. Wuzzie learned of its uses from Mattie; she still prepares paint for herself and her

Gambling was a favorite pastime among the Indians, and scenes like this were common to the white settlers.

friends. One day we went to a bright red outcrop on the mountain to fill boxes and bags with the raw, brick-colored earth, and I watched her make it into balls. This was the same quarry where Jack Wilson, the famous Ghost Dance leader, gathered the paint which he mailed to his followers all over the United States.[28]

Wuzzie's first work in the white people's homes was ironing towels. She was so little she had to stand on a box to reach the ironing board. Sometimes she watched a small band of sheep, and the white lady gave her ten cents a day, which she always

27

used to buy candy at Jim Richards' store. She was a "big girl" when her mother died, and she was taken to the Indian school at Stewart, eighty miles away. She was at the school only half a year when there was an epidemic of measles and some of the children died. Fearing that Wuzzie would also die, her father came with a horse and buggy and took her home. "That is why I never got my schooling," she said. So Wuzzie's education in the Old Ways continued under her grandmother.

After leaving school Wuzzie lived in the new town of Fallon, because "all of the Indians go to Fallon when Jim Richards move his store there." They lived in tents, rag-covered frames of willow, and one-room, board-and-batten shacks on the outskirts of town. Then one of their group died of smallpox, and the townspeople insisted that the Indians move their community further away.

By this time Stovepipe had died and Mattie was getting very old. Wuzzie and her sister-cousin Mamie took care of Mattie while they both worked at a "Chinaman's restaurant." Wuzzie tells how, in May, 1910, a fire started in a nearby saloon. The restaurant and many other buildings went up in smoke that night. There were two monkeys in the bar. One was burned to death but the other escaped and amused Mattie all summer in the cottonwood trees above the Indians' gambling area. After the fire the "Chinaman" went away, and Wuzzie started working on a ranch.

Mattie died in the mountains while they were all out gathering pinenuts one fall. Wuzzie said she was not sick—just tired. She thought that Mattie was "maybe 80, 90 years old." In a box of old negatives which had come to me were many pictures of Indians taken by Mr. Roly Ham, an early Nevada photographer. One photo, copyrighted in 1902, shows two women seated on the ground near a scattering of Indian houses typical of the early days of transition. The younger woman is dignified and a little resentful of the photographer's intrusion; the older woman, fanning away the flies with a bit of cloth, is weary and resigned. Wuzzie stared at the photograph for a long time. Then she said quietly, "Him, my aunt; and him, my grandma." This, then, was the little old lady, Mattie, wife of Stovepipe, to whom we are indirectly indebted for much of the material in this book.

Maggie, wife of One-eye Pete,
and Mattie, wife of Stovepipe.

In the Manner of
the Old Ones

In the Manner of
the Old Ones

HARVESTING PINENUTS

In the Old Days the pinenutting season was one of reverence, contentment, and good-fellowship. Cousins who had not seen each other for months set up camps side by side. Friends met friends and exchanged bits of news as they moved from tree to tree. Word of births and deaths was greeted with laughs or wails that rang through the forest. Jokes were told, girls were courted, and songs were sung. Naked, cream-colored babies tumbled in the pine needles, cutting their teeth on pine sticks. Boys climbed pine trees to shake down the cones; their lithe bodies, black with pitch, became blacker when they rubbed themselves with dust so they would not stick to their rabbitskin blankets at night.

Old women sat in contented groups beating nuts from the huge baskets of cones which the young people carried to them. Old men tended their traps or puttered in the sun, enjoying the fragrance of pine and sage and pitchy smoke that rolled down the mountain like water. The ancient ones, spent by the long walk, slept deeply, vaguely aware that their next journey would be along the Milky Way, the Dusty Road where there would be "no more hungry, no more cold."

Wuzzie told of the way of her people: "When we come to a pinenut place we talk to the ground and the mountain and everything. We ask to feel good and strong. We ask for cool breeze to sleep at night. The pinenuts belong to the mountain so we ask the mountain for some of its pinenuts to take home and eat. The water is the mountain's juice. It comes out of the mountain, so we ask the mountain for some of its juice to make us feel good and happy. Just the old people do this. The young people don't care, they just walk on the mountain anyhow."[29]

The single-leaf piñons are the typical pines of the desert mountains of Nevada, Utah, Arizona, and southeastern California. They are scrubby, round trees producing tons of pinenuts annually which the Indians harvested in the fall. These nuts, virtually the only nuts used by the Indians of Western Nevada, are about the size of olive pits, and lie in pairs behind each cone-scale in the tangerine-sized cones.

By the time of the first frost, when the cones were bursting, all of the Basin Indians could be found in the pinenut forests, gathering, roasting, eating, and storing as many nuts as they could. This food was by far the most delicious in their diet—the

Pinenuts, a favorite food of the Indians, are harvested in large quantities in the fall. When ripe, the pinecones open like full-blown flowers.

The long stick used to hook and beat cones from the trees is made of willows tied together.

easiest to harvest and store, extremely nourishing, and often the most abundant.

Men beat the trees with long poles, causing showers of cones, nuts, twigs, and pitch to fall on the women and children as they gleaned the nuts from the ground.

Today, canvas and sheets are spread under the trees to catch the nuts. Burlap sacks and flour sacks are used for storing them, but the conical burden baskets and the winnowing trays of the Old Days are still the most practical implements for carrying and cleaning.

A beating pole was made by splicing two long willow sticks together tip to tip. A short stick was lashed at an angle to one end of the pole to hook cones from the trees. The baskets were made of willow too—coarsely woven to sieve the trash, the needles, pitch, and twigs, from the nuts.

The gathering started at break of day. Whole families moved among the trees, stopping wherever a pine was found bending low with its load of cones. Women carried their pinenut baskets from straps across

Tools for the pinenut harvest;
conical burden baskets and winnowing trays
still in use today date from
early Paiute history.

their foreheads; the men took their poles and water jugs in their hands; youths bounded ahead like wild things to search out good pines; and girls hauled the loaded baskets back to camp, where their grandmothers and aunts sat together cleaning the nuts for roasting.

When the sun was high and warm the Indians napped, stretched out on the bare ground, until the shadows lengthened and the chill breeze that stirred the pines brought to them the fragrance of nuts roasting in camp.

Around the campfire the grandfathers told children the story of when all of the Indians had been animals, how Crow had smelled the pinenut roasting in the North, and how all of the animals had gone there to get it. Before that, he said, the Indians had had no pinenuts.

In the fall of 1957 at Desert Creek in the Sweetwater Mountains in Nevada, Wuzzie George gathered nuts to make pinenut soup.

Wuzzie cleaned clinging debris from the nuts before roasting them, taking special care to remove the lumps of pitch which would burn the basket during the roasting process.

Shoveling hot coals from the breakfast fire onto the small, brown pinenuts in the winnowing tray, she began immediately to bounce and turn them, keeping them in constant motion to protect the basket from becoming scorched.

When the nuts hissed and popped, somewhat like popcorn, she knew they were cooked. This first roasting leaves the meats soft and translucent.

*1
Wuzzie's winnowing basket
is used for cleaning pitch and needles
from the nuts before the roasting.*

*2
The coals, glowing brightly,
are placed on the nuts.*

*3
The hot coals and nuts
are tossed continuously.*

With a few quick motions she separated the coals from the nuts and flipped them over the edge of the basket. Any black fragments that remained, she picked out with her fingers.

Then the nuts were placed on a board or flat rock and, using either a mano or a huller (grinding stones held in the hand), she cracked the thin shells with a gentle crushing motion. So skilled was she in the shelling process that scarcely a nut was crushed or left unshelled. Occasionally she paused to remove a bit of charcoal, but there was very little remaining.

4
*After the nuts are roasted,
the coals are flipped over the edge
of the basket.*

5
*Small remaining fragments of charcoal
are removed by hand.*

6
*Like the Old People, Wuzzie used
a stone huller, but instead of
a stone metate, she used a board.*

7
*The huller is rubbed gently over the nuts
cracking the shells but not the kernels.*

The nuts were returned to the winnowing basket where they were separated from the empty shells. With a softly spoken prayer she called on the wind to help her with the winnowing. But the wind failed to come on call, so she blew the last of the shells from the basket.

There was the tranquility of lapping waves in the rhythm of the winnowing. The slanting winter sun cast shadows of the nuts on her cheeks, and overhead, flocks of pine-jays talked to each other. Wuzzie said that one jay in the flock, which had a different voice, was a doctor for the pinenuts.

After the nuts were clean and ready for the second roasting, hot coals were again put over them. The nuts and coals were flipped in a manner that kept them not only moving up and down, but rotating around in the basket. When the blackened nuts became hard and brittle, the last of the ashes and debris were removed by more winnowing.

8
Wuzzie next winnowed the empty shells from the nutmeats.

9
Then she blew the last shell fragments from the basket.

10
*The nutmeats are clean and ready
for the second roasting.*

11
*Fresh coals harden and blacken
the nutmeats during the final roasting.*

To clean the nuts, Wuzzie ground a handful of the meats into a gray powder which she shook over the remaining nuts. Then she sprinkled a little water over the whole mass, making a paste which she rolled over the nuts. The paste, acting much like a gum rubber eraser, cleaned the meats and gathered up the last bits of shell and charcoal into small black balls.

Wuzzie said that the Old People rolled the little black balls into the form of a burden basket and put a tiny spike in the bottom. This they gave to the children, telling them that it was the pinenut basket of the Old Woman who carried away children who cried at night. Indian children played with the balls of paste much as children today play with dough when their mothers are baking.

The manos and metates with which the women ground the nuts and seeds were not carried to and from the pinenut areas because of their weight. Instead, they were placed in the crotches of juniper trees or were neatly stacked and left in camp to be used the following year. After the appearance of white men, the highly-prized heavy stone tools were buried to protect them from theft.

12
To clean the nuts, Wuzzie starts
by grinding a few of them into flour.

13
She made a paste by sprinkling water
over the nuts and flour.

14
Next she rolled the pinenut paste
into balls under the palms of her hands.

15
The soft balls of paste
clean the meats by gathering up
the bits of charcoal and ash.

16
Ground between a mano and metate,
the nuts are converted into flour
a few at a time.

Pinenuts are a highly concentrated food, rich in protein. The Indians ate them raw, roasted, or made into soup. Roasted pinenuts, cracked and eaten like peanuts, do not have enough bulk to satisfy, so the Indians ground them and made them into a delicious, saltless gruel which could be eaten hot or cold.

Placing a few nuts on the back of her metate, Wuzzie moved the meats forward a few at a time with each pushing stroke. The flour was quite fine and of a creamy gray color.

Wuzzie used a paper bag to catch the flour; her grandmother would have used a fine-woven winnowing basket.

Meanwhile, Jimmy had been cleaning the bark from a short sturdy stick for her to use in stirring the pinenut soup.

Substituting a bucket for the cooking basket used long ago, she mixed the meal into a thick paste and then thinned it to the desired consistency. Wuzzie said her grandmother told her always to use a stick to mix the soup. Her grandmother knew a woman who "used her hands, and pretty soon she died."

17
In the Old Days, a fine-woven winnowing basket would have been used instead of paper to catch the flour.

18
*Jimmy carved a temporary stirring stick
for Wuzzie to use in making soup.*

19
*Water from a mountain spring
is added slowly to the pinenut soup
to thin it to the right consistency.*

20
*The soup can be heated
for eating if desired.*

A BOAT OF CATTAIL AND TULE

For the people of the marshes, the Cattail-eaters, the tules and cattails furnished not only such basic essentials as food, shelter, and clothing, but the raw materials for many other necessities—boats, bags, decoys, and matting.

Cattails are easily identified by their handsome brown velvet stalks. Tiny seeds form a tubular sheath around tightly-packed, silken threads. When broken loose the seeds journey far on passing breezes, often settling to grow in wet, marshy areas.

The leaves are long, slender, and flat—tender when green, but tough enough to make rope after they turn brown in the fall. The Indians found many uses for them. They were braided and twisted; they were woven and matted. They were used for bedding and blankets, for lining storage pits and roasting pits, and for tying all manner of things together. For the Indians, they served the purposes that thongs, tape, and wire do in our society.

Together with the cattails, the tules grew in dense, gray-green clumps that covered acre after acre of the marshes. Tules are tall, round reeds that bear a plume of seeds near the tip. Being pithy, they are buoyant and so are used for making boats and decoys. Unlike the cattails, the tules are tough when green, but brittle when dry.

As long as anyone could remember, the Cattail-eaters had made boats of tules tied together with ropes of cattail. They used

1
After gathering bundles of tules,
Jimmy waded deep into the marshes.

these boats to gather mudhen eggs or to drive flightless molting ducks onto shore. The tule boats were not strong enough to last more than one season, so even Indians of later times had ample opportunity to learn how to build these balsa-like crafts. As a boy, Jimmy George had made them many times, and now for me, he made another. The only tool he needed to build his boat was a knife. In ages before, the Old People had used sickles made from the shoulder blades of deer, or thin sheets of slate with fluted edges.

First he cut two large bundles of tules for the body of the boat and he and Wuzzie carried them in from the marsh on their backs in the manner of the Old People. After gathering the tules, Jimmy located cattails in another area some distance away. Wading into the water where the tallest cattails grew, Jimmy gathered a supply and carried them to the shore. He chose those leaves which had not been broken by the winter storms; they would be used to make ropes to tie the boat together.

2
He gathered cattail leaves
to use in making rope.

To toughen the cattails, Jimmy threw an armload into shallow water and pushed them down with the bottom of a bucket. When they were thoroughly soaked. Wuzzie and Jimmy selected the leaves that would make strong rope. Using two small bundles of cattails, they lapped the tips of the leaves far enough to make a rope of the desired length. After twisting, they had a short piece of rope which two strong men could not have broken. When it was dry it would not easily unwind.

3
*The cattail leaves are made
tough and pliable by soaking.*

4
*Only the unbroken cattail leaves
are selected.*

5
*Jimmy and Wuzzie twist the leaves together
to make a strong rope.*

The boats were made of two bundles of tules tied with ropes of twisted cattails. Five loops of the cattail rope were enough to hold each bundle. Instead of being knotted, the ends were twisted and tucked into the bundle.

With Wuzzie's help, Jimmy tied the two bundles together at the stern. Then, while Wuzzie drew the prow of the boat upward, Jimmy bound the tips with more cattail rope.

When the bundles were entirely secure, Jimmy trimmed the uneven lengths of tules from the prow of the boat with his knife. The stern of the boat was also trimmed and shaped to a rounded end.

6
Jimmy ties a bundle of tules together with his cattail rope. The ends of the rope are twisted and tucked in.

9
The prow is formed by drawing the tips of the tule bundles upward, and tying them in place.

7
A second bundle is made in the same manner.

8
Wuzzie helps Jimmy tie the two bundles together.

Next Jimmy made a gunwale of cattail leaves. Wuzzie said that cattails were used instead of tules because they were stronger. The Old People used the gunwale to keep the harvest of duck and mudhen eggs from rolling off. Boats were also used by the hunters to carry home their fish and game.

To make the gunwale, Jimmy and Wuzzie tied a bundle of cattails to the prow of the boat and another to the stern. These were then secured along the sides with twisted cattail ropes.

10
The ragged ends of the prow and stern . . .

11
. . . are trimmed with a knife.

12
A gunwale is needed to keep eggs, game, and weapons from sliding off.

13
Cattails are used for the gunwale because they are stronger than tules.

14
Starting at the back, a second bundle of cattails is tied to the boat.

15
The ends are brought forward and bound to the front half of the gunwale.

When the boat was completed, Jimmy stepped in the center to form a deeper hollow. The finished boat was eight-and-a-half feet long but so light that it could easily be lifted with one hand.

The prime use for a boat of this size was to carry game and weapons while the hunter waded or swam, pushing the boat ahead of him. However, it easily held a man's weight, as Jimmy demonstrated by poling

16
Jimmy deepens the hollow in the boat with his foot.

17
The completed boat could be lifted with one hand.

18
Jimmy poles his tule boat across the marshes in the Old Way.

across the marsh. "Not use a paddle," Jimmy explained, "just use stick to push." Jimmy had never seen a double-ended boat, but sometimes larger boats were made which would carry two or more men.

After the boat had been in the water for a few hours, it was very heavy. Tule boats never sank even after they had absorbed much water, Jimmy said. When not in use they were pulled onto the shore where the hot desert sun soon dried them out and restored their former buoyancy.

MAKING A DUCK DECOY

The marsh was a storehouse of food for the Indians—seeds, stalks, eggs, muskrats, fish, and birds. There were fleets of white pelicans that furled and unfurled their wings like sails; ducks that came in for noisy landings in pairs; small flotillas of coots—black of body and white of face—that made converging V-shaped wakes as they ran across the water on their paddle-feet; grebes that glided through the marshes raising their white periscope necks above the water, calling to each other in squeaky-windmill voices.

Indians, moving among the reeds, their

48

black hair dusted with golden cattail pollen, were as much a part of the marsh scene as the killdeer ("Water-legs"), the bittern, ("Looks-at-the-sun"), or the haze of May flies that beat on naked brown bodies like a sandstorm.

Duck decoys were used by the Indians in the same way they are used by modern hunters today.[30] The hunter with his tule basket of decoys over his shoulder, and bow and arrows in his hand, hunted all of the birds, unrestricted by game laws and bag limits. The best kind of duckskin for a decoy, Wuzzie said, was the canvasback. The hunter set out his decoys and ruffled the water with his fingertips to imitate the sound of feeding ducks. The decoys attracted not only ducks, but mudhens—and the Indians ate them both.

The only materials that Jimmy needed to make a duck decoy came from the marshes and the nearby desert. From the marshes he collected about fifteen very large tules, an armload of cattails, and a freshly killed duck. From the greasewood bushes in the desert, he gathered slender hardwood sticks about a foot long.

He began the construction of the decoy by doubling three or four tules around the middle of a larger bundle of tules and binding them together with a small cattail rope. This would become the back and tail of the decoy.

Beginning with the right side of the larger bundle of tules, he started twining small bunches together with ropes of cattail leaves. This spread the tules out like a fan. Then he tied the cattail rope to the tail section. With Wuzzie's help in twisting rope, he wove the other end in the same manner.

1
*Jimmy is starting to make the tule frame
for a duck decoy.*

2
Using a cattail rope,
he wove the tules into a fan shape,
forming the right hand side of the frame.

3
The side of the decoy
is tied to the tailpiece.

4
The left side of the decoy
is fashioned in the same manner.

Wuzzie helped Jimmy bend the fan until all the tules were pointing in the same direction. In the center he made a hollow with his fist. With a piece of cattail rope, he tied the body together and trimmed the tail so that it pointed upward.

Then he cut off the wings of the duck and discarded them. They were not missed since the scapulars appeared to be wings in the finished product. Next he cut off the legs, split the duck down the breast, and removed the flesh through the narrow slit.

5
With Wuzzie's help, Jimmy pulls
the sides and back together.

6
He punched a hollow into the bottom of the frame with his fist.

7
*Before tying the tail,
he pulled the long ends
of the tules together.*

8
*Next he trimmed the tail
so that it pointed upward.*

9
*He removed the wings and feet
of a freshly killed duck.*

10
*By removing the flesh
through a slit in the breast,
the duckskin is left intact.*

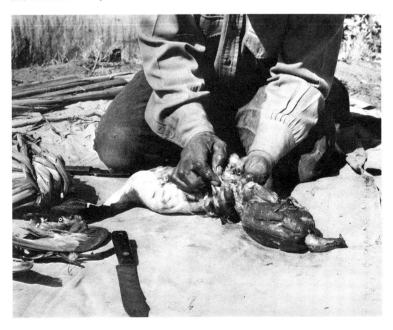

To make stuffing for the neck, Jimmy shredded a handful of cattails, twisted them, bent them double, and forced them into the empty neckskin of the duck. Then, pointing one of the longer greasewood sticks, he pushed it up the neck and out the top of the head. With the bottom end of the stick pushed down into the tule frame, the head was held erect.

Next he stretched the duckskin over the tule frame and pinned it in place with short twigs of greasewood. The stick which protruded from the head was broken off and the feathers smoothed over the stub.

11
Cattails are shredded
to make a stuffing for the neck.

12
The shredded cattails are twisted,
bent double, and inserted into the neck.

13
A hard, greasewood stick
is thrust into the neck
and out the top of the head . . .

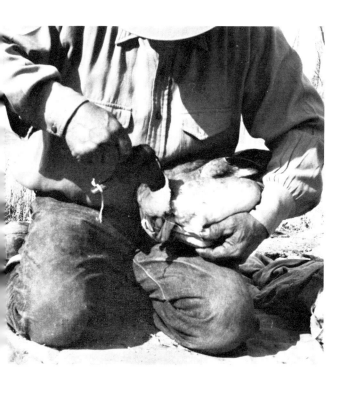

14
*. . . and is then
pushed back down into the tule frame
to hold the head upright.*

15
*Jimmy stretches the skin
over the tule frame . . .*

16
*. . . and pins it down around the edges
with short greasewood twigs.*

With the bill tied shut and the edge of the skin fastened to the frame with greasewood sticks, the decoy was ready to set afloat. A cache of similar decoys dating from centuries ago was excavated from a nearby cave in 1924.

17
Before launching the decoy,
Jimmy tied the bill and
smoothed the feathers.

18
In the water,
it looked more like a pet duck
than a tule-stuffed skin.

CORDAGE

Lacking nails, bolts, and screws, and having little to use for adhesives, the Paiute Indians tied their world together. They tied their wood and willows in bundles to carry them into camp; they tied small game onto their waist bands; they tied the tules to make boats, and cattails to make houses; they tied babies in baskets, and arrowheads to shafts. They used cords in place of buttons and safety pins, to make traps, to catch fish and hang them to dry. In addition to the tough rope of cattails and sagebrush bark, they made strong string of sinew and human hair. They also used supple young willow withes for tying. But the finest cordage of all was made of Indian hemp, or dogbane.

Common in much of the Basin, hemp grows in moist soil along the banks of streams or where the water table is high. Each year fresh, green stalks push up from the roots, grow shoulder high, form thin pods like milkweed, and dry up in the fall, accumulating for many seasons into a maze. The new stalks are reddish brown and with each succeeding year they become more faded and shaggy. Those stalks which had stood in the field for more than one year were considered too weak to use.

Resembling both a willow and a milkweed, the stalk is made up of three parts: first, a thin outer skin; second, the long tough fibers; and third, a pithy tube which is hollow in the center.

Areas where the plants grew tallest and developed the fewest branches were well known to the Indians. At one such place, Johnny and Nina Dunn cut several armloads of hemp and Johnny sorted out the long, straight stalks and trimmed off the small side branches.

The thin, reddish skin first had to be scraped off with a knife (long ago, a crescent-shaped bit of obsidian was used). Then the stalk was pressed between the thumb and forefinger to crack it lengthwise from the tip to about six inches from the base. Johnny said that teeth were somtimes used to crack the stalk, but he had never heard of it being pounded with a rock.

1
Indian hemp with tall straight stalks was sought for the manufacture of cordage.

2
Johnny scrapes off the thin red bark with a knife.

3
The hollow stalk is cracked between thumbs and fingers along nearly its whole length.

The stalk was split lengthwise, exposing the tubular, pithy center. An unbroken section was often left at the base, like a handle, to keep the fibers from becoming tangled while they were stored.

Holding the pithy side of the split stalk against his left wrist, Johnny ran his right hand along it, bending it at intervals against his left arm. This process cracked the pith in short sections and loosened it from the fiber. Both halves of the stalk were treated in the same manner.

The dangling bits of pith were scraped or brushed from the fibers with the fingernails, and the fibers were separated by gentle rubbing. If there was any moisture in the plants, Johnny said, the pith would not break easily.

4
Johnny pushed half the stem aside to crack the pith into short sections against his arm.

5
The pith on the second half is also broken.

6
The bits of pith are removed by shaking and scraping, leaving only the fibers which are then rubbed gently to separate them from each other.

After a supply of fiber was prepared, Johnny started making a two-ply cord. First, he rolled a few fibers along his leg with the palm of his hand, using a pushing motion. When he had finished about two feet of string, he started the second ply. Then with the flat of his hand, he twisted the two plies together with a rolling stroke toward his body. Thus the working distance between the raw fiber and the completed cord was less than two feet—one stroke pushing out and one stroke pulling back.

When new fibers were needed to increase the length, they were spliced in a few at a time. The process was repeated again and again until the string was the required length. As it was completed it was wound on a stick. Johnny had never made the fine cordage that was used in tying nets, but he had made heavier cord to rig his harpoons. Edna Jones said that her grandfather, Captain Wasson, wore no clothes when he was making string because the fibers rolled better on bare skin.

7
To make the two-ply cordage used in tying nets, a few fibers were rolled under the palm of the hand with a pushing motion.

8
The second strand was twisted in the same manner.

Cordage made from Indian hemp probably reached its greatest perfection in the manufacture of netting for trapping rabbits, ducks, fish, etc. This handsome rabbit net, as nearly as can be traced, was made by Captain Wasson of Walker Lake.[31] Originally it was over three hundred feet long. Even though his other possessions were burned, according to custom, when Captain Wasson died, the net was cut in half, and one half given to each of his two daughters. One portion was lost. The other half was put away and saved. The string in this net, about the size of kitchen twine, is so uniform that it is hard to believe that it was made by hand.

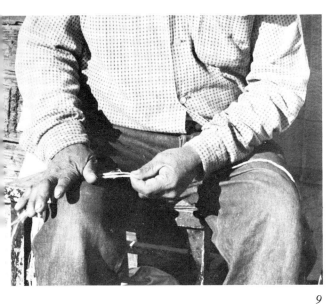

9
Then, to make a two-ply cord, both strands were rolled together with a pulling motion.

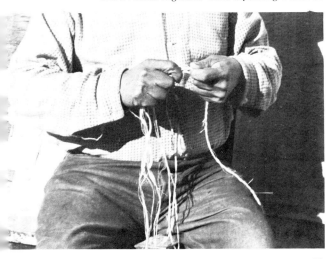

10
When Johnny reached the end of the fibers, new strands were spliced into the cord . . .

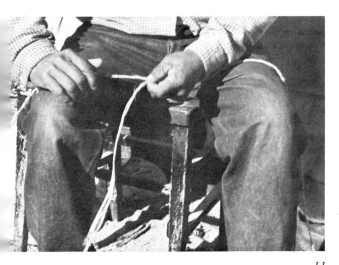

11
. . . and the twisting continued, forming an unbroken string.

12
Captain Wasson's rabbit net was of exquisite workmanship. The mesh was just large enough to catch a rabbit behind the ears when it tried to force its way through. The entire net was tied with a chain stitch which was repeated until the net was short enough for storage.

FISHING AND HARPOONS

In the Old Days, fish of many species were found in the waters of the Great Basin. The small mountain creeks carried native trout while chubs, minnows, and shiners were taken from the rivers and sloughs of the low country. Pyramid, Winnemucca, and Walker lakes were food-rich with a large variety of fish. The most desirable was the huge, black-spotted cutthroat trout found only in the tributaries and the remnant lakes of ancient Lake Lahontan. In late winter and again in the spring they spawned in great numbers in the Truckee and Walker rivers, providing a welcome bounty when other foods were scarce.

The cui-ui sucker, a fish of mysterious origin, furnished tons of dried meat for the Indians. In April and May the cui-ui left

Pyramid and Winnemucca lakes to make their spawning migration up the Truckee River. When the tiny fry hatched they returned to the depths of the saline lakes. As far as is known, man has never seen an immature cui-ui in its natural habitat.

Three or four years later, when the fish were about a foot long, they answered the beckoning of springtime and the rising fresh waters of the flooding Truckee River and moved in great, dense schools along the bottom of the lake into the mouth of the river, swimming upstream until they could no longer push their blunt heads against the swift current. Their number was so great that they often jammed together two and three feet deep. At times whole schools became stranded, thrashing helplessly in the shallow water; some were even pushed out onto the sand bars to die. Gulls, cormorants, pelicans, and Indians swooped down upon them.

Men caught while women cleaned. Fish were cut open and hung over hastily-erected drying racks. Anything was used that would hold the fish open to the air to dry—willow frames, piles of brush, roofs of sunshades, bushes, and later, wire mesh. Brush was piled on top of the fish to protect them from the coyotes and magpies while the Indians left the catch to dry and moved on to the next concentration of fish along the lower reaches of the Truckee.

In the early days, when every morsel of food was conserved, the entire fish was saved. The head was cut off, split, and hung up to dry. Clusters of fish eggs were pulled apart, spread out on winnowing trays, and later stored in bags. The entrails were also cleaned and dried. The meat, eyes, tongues, and bits of flesh from the heads became finger food. In winter the dried fish—heads, meat, entrails, and eggs— were often ground and boiled to make a soup.

Before the coming of the white man, Pyramid Lake Indians set nets in the mouth of the Truckee. Later, they learned from the white man to fish off the delta with drag hooks thrown by hand.

With the coming of irrigation and the diversion of water for power, Winnemucca Lake became dry and the Truckee River began to flow so thinly across its broad,

1
Fishing at Pyramid Lake for cui-ui
in the delta of the Truckee River.

sandy delta that the cui-ui could rarely cross it. When they felt the spawning urge, they amassed at the mouth of the river, churning about on the silty bottom in a futile attempt to migrate upstream. Circling pelicans signaled their arrival and the Indians spread the word swiftly through the community that the cui-ui were running. Soon, fishermen, young and old, carrying three-pronged drag hooks hung in a series on a weighted line, gathered on the shore. With a lassoing motion, they threw the hooks as far as possible into the lake and then dragged them along the bottom with quick, sharp jerks, snagging a fish with nearly every cast.

Today casting poles are replacing the snag lines and the cui-ui population is shrinking, but the Indians continue to make a holiday of the annual run during the warm, sunny days of late April and early May.

FISHING

The cui-ui has a pleasant flavor but its flesh is laced with hundreds of thin Y-shaped bones. Only a four-inch square fillet near the head is boneless. Today only this

2
Cui-ui are caught by the Indians during the spring spawning migration.

3
Present-day Indians avoid the numerous bones by saving only the cui-ui fillets.

fillet is saved; the remainder of the fish is dragged off and buried.

Katy Frazier had always dried fish in the manner of the Old People when they caught more than they could use. Working on the shore of the lake where myriads of tiny white snail shells formed a scalloped border at the edge of the water, she first removed the large, ugly heads. She cut the cui-ui down the back on both sides of the vertebrae, enabling her to remove the entrails and the backbone at the same time. Then she trimmed off the fins and, finally, washed the fish thoroughly before setting it out to dry.

4
Katy Frazier begins cleaning the cui-ui by cutting off the large heads.

5
Next she cuts them down the back . . .

6
. . . and pulls the entrails and vertabrae out together.

7
She cuts off the fins and washes the fish in the lake.

To dry the cui-ui, Harry Winnemucca cut slashes across the fish to keep them from curling, tied their tails together, and hung them up with the flesh side out. Sometimes they were propped open to the air with little sticks. Early explorers often saw jerky and fish hanging from the willow frames of grass houses and from racks nearby.

HARPOONS

Many ingenious methods of fishing were used by the Paiute Indians. Weirs were made by driving willow stakes into the river bottom to support removable wicker frames. These frames detained the spawning fish

8
Harry Winnemucca slashes the cui-ui to keep them from curling while they dry.

9
The cui-ui are tied in pairs by the tails and hung in the open air together with jerky.

while the Indians scooped them out with dip nets. Clusters of L-shaped hooks of greasewood or bone, baited with the black-and-white grubs that lived in the greasewood roots, were hung on hemp string. Nets of exquisite workmanship were set in the rivers and lakes. Old women wading in the sloughs used coarse-woven winnowing baskets to dip the minnows up onto the banks to dry for winter food. The men made harpoons of bone, quill, hemp, willow, pitch, and charcoal to spear the big river fish and the lake trout.

Johnny Dunn, who belonged to a well-known family of fishermen at Pyramid Lake, told how harpoons were made long ago. He had made many in his lifetime. To demonstrate, he first melted a small amount of pine pitch by holding it near a tiny fire of chips and twigs. When the pitch became soft, he added bits of charcoal and then ground the mixture together. He explained that the charcoal gave an extra hardness to the pitch. To fashion a spear point he sharpened a sliver of bone from the leg of a deer. After the advent of the white man, the Indians often substituted nails for such bone slivers.

10
Johnny Dunn builds a small fire
to melt pine pitch for use
in making a harpoon.

11
The charcoal and hot pitch
are ground together
between two rocks.

Johnny wrapped one end of a hemp string tightly around the center of the bone point, leaving the other end long enough so that it could later be tied to the pole. To keep the string from sliding off, he daubed it with hot pitch. The point was to be held to a slender foreshaft of greasewood (which could easily be replaced if broken by a large fish). To hold the point to the foreshaft he split a pelican quill lengthwise, making a housing so the point could slip off easily after entering the fish.

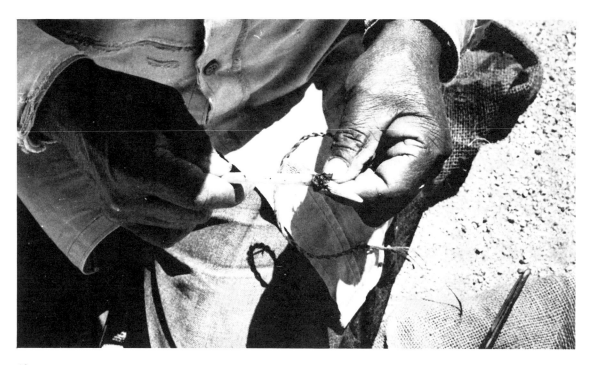

12
The end of a hemp string is wound
around the center of the bone point. A small stick
is used to daub on hot pitch
to cement the string in place.

13
Johnny split a pelican quill . . .

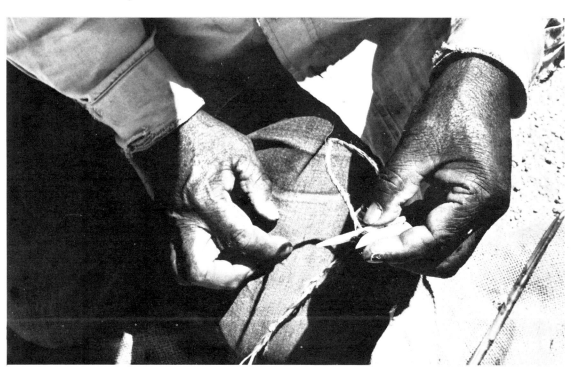

He wrapped the quill around the point and the foreshaft, binding them together with more string. Reheating the pitch he cemented the string to the point and quill, and as the pitch cooled he smoothed the roughness out with his fingers.

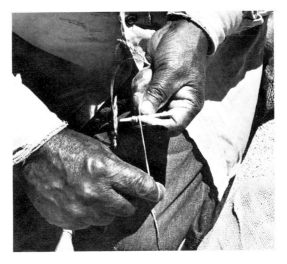

14
. . . and fastened it to the bone point to make a slipcase for the foreshaft.

15
With the foreshaft in the slipcase he finishes binding the quill to the bone point.

16
Johnny reheated the pitch and applied it to the string.

17
As the pitch cooled, he molded it smoothly over the string and point.

Then Johnny trimmed a long willow pole on which to mount the foreshaft. With more string of his own making, he bound the foreshaft to the pole in two places. When the string from the point was tied to the pole, the harpoon was complete, and the only articles of white man's culture that had been used were a knife and a match.

Johnny always carried extra harpoon points and foreshafts. He said that the best place to spear fish was where the river flowed over a white, sandy bottom because there the big, dark fish could be seen more easily. Some men squatted on the bank, harpoons in hand, watching for the fish which were struggling up the river, while other men stood around a fire talking and waiting for their turn. When a fish was sighted, the Indian lowered the tip of the harpoon into the water and let it drift with the current like a piece of driftwood until it was opposite the swimming fish. Then he gave the harpoon a quick thrust. Often, Johnny said, the point would pass completely through the body. The bone tip would then slip off the end of the foreshaft and, since it was tied in the middle, turn crosswise, holding the fish securely to the willow pole.

18
He trimmed a sturdy willow
for a spear pole and bound the foreshaft
to it in two places.

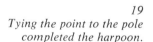

19
Tying the point to the pole
completed the harpoon.

20
Johnny is ready
to go spear-fishing.

ARROWS AND DEADFALLS

Hunting was a man's domain, and the Paiute man used most of the devices known to primitive hunters the world over—bows and arrows, spears and snares, fire and water, bait and poison, and the rat stick.[32] He made pitfalls[33] and deadfalls, disguises and decoys, nets and blinds.[34] He sang, danced, prayed, and painted himself with red ochre, and enlisted every supernatural power he knew. A good hunter was fleet of foot, keen of eye, and abundantly endowed with patience. He provided a variety of meat without which his family would have gone hungry.

While the women moved from valley to valley harvesting the ripening seeds, the men harvested the game. The hunter left camp at the "yellow light" of dawn when the small rodents came out in search of food. Along the river bottoms he hunted porcupines[35] where they stripped bark from the willows, and shot cottontails as they darted among the sagebrush. By the marshes he brought down the ducks, geese, and mudhens which were lured within range by his decoys. In the desert he shot jackrabbits, ground squirrels, and badgers with his bow and arrows. He set a line of deadfalls and pitfalls for birds, kangaroo rats, and chipmunks, and revisited it daily. He hunted nearly everything that moved.

When the shimmering heat of midday drove the animals under cover, he returned home with his catch. After the game was quickly cooked and hungrily eaten, the hunter chipped new arrows, mended his nets, or slept in a bit of shade until the cool of evening again brought the animals from hiding.

When the family moved to the hills for pinenuts, the hunter reset the string of deadfalls which he had left behind the previous year. Then he went to hunt marmots among the huge boulder piles. With his bow and arrows he sat motionless in the warm morning sun until the hoary head of a rockchuck appeared from its burrow. If he were fortunate, he shot it through the eye; if not, the marmot would be gone before he could reach it. He also hunted porcupines in the mountains, but they tasted strongly of the pine bark on which they fed. Occasionally, an especially skilled hunter brought home a deer or a mountain sheep, and there would be great joy in camp. The deer meat was shared with all. However, the hunter himself avoided eating the heart. He believed that if he ate the heart, his own heart would beat fast the next time he drew his bow on a deer, and thus spoil his aim.

He usually hunted alone except during the rabbit drives and the antelope hunts. Little is remembered about antelope hunts, because the antelope disappeared when the cattle were brought in.[36] The Old People recall, however, that an antelope-hunt leader, through the power of a dream, determined the best time, place, and procedure for the hunt. When the Indians had assembled, they usually sang and danced for five days until they had charmed the overly curious antelope herd into the range of their arrows.

Details of the rabbit drive also are nearly forgotten. When the Old Ones died, their rabbit nets were buried with them, and the young people did not have the patience for learning to make new ones. All that re-

mains of the old hunting practices is an occasional skill remembered by some grandfather from the days of his youth, or an arrowhead found by chance on the desert floor.

These projectile points made from stone are the most striking and best-known artifacts to survive from the Old Days. The oldest points, large and crudely formed, were probably attached to spears which were thrown by hand. With the development of the atlatl—a hooked stick which acted as an extension for the arm—the spear could be thrown with greater force. When, some two thousand years ago, the bow and arrow came into use in the Great Basin, arrowheads became smaller and of more delicate workmanship; most of them were made from black, glassy obsidian.

Arrow-making, like bow-hunting, was a man's job. Often the obsidian had to be carried great distances. To avoid carrying excess weight, blanks were usually broken from the massive rock at the quarry site. Keenly aware that obsidian from different localities had different fracture planes, the Indians struck large flakes from obsidian boulders at the precise angle to produce the best spalls and the fewest rejects. Chipping stations found today on vantage points overlooking game trails suggest that the hunter often used the hours of patient waiting to make his arrowheads, leaving behind the defective points and tiny refuse chips.

1
By striking an obsidian boulder
at the proper angle, thin spalls
are obtained from which the arrowheads
can be made.

ARROWHEADS

With the coming of the gun, bows and arrows disappeared. Today arrowheads are made only rarely, as objects of beauty and not as weapons. Levi Frazier, Jr., learned to make them from an older friend who, in turn, had learned from his own grandfather. He uses tools identical to those used by the Paiutes for many generations—a piece of buckskin to protect the palm of his hand from the splintering obsidian, and a deer-antler tip for flaking. To the Old People's tools he added a common nail to make the notches for hafting the arrow to the shaft. Levi did not know what the Old People used, but he could not remove fine chips with a dull-pointed antler.

2
*Levi Frazier, Jr., chips flakes
from the bottom side of the arrowhead
by pressing the antler down
against the sharp edge of the obsidian.*

3
*The angle of the antler to the flake
governs the length of the chip
that is removed.*

4
*Tiny notches for hafting
the arrowhead to the shaft
are made with a nail.*

For arrow shafts, Jimmy George used straight rosewood sticks or stems of the same cane from which the women gathered honey-dew. He bound the feathers and arrowheads to the shafts with thin threads of deer sinew soaked in water until they were soft. Often he decorated his arrows with red pigment because he believed the paint had special power. His quivers were made either of bobcat or fox skin molded into a tube and tied at the bottom. Jimmy had hunted rabbits with bow and arrow when he was young, but he preferred a gun when he could afford ammunition.

5
Sinew, the tendons in the back of a deer,
is soaked and stripped into thread
for binding arrowheads and feathers onto shafts.

6
Jimmy's quiver, made of bobcat skin,
is filled with sturdy cane arrows.

DEADFALLS

Besides being a good worker in the white man's hayfields, Jimmy was a good hunter. He knew how to set deadfalls in the same manner described by the explorer Captain J. H. Simpson more than a hundred years ago, in 1859.[37] According to Simpson the rock was "supported by a kind of figure 4, made as it ordinarily is for traps, except that, instead of a piece of wood, a string is used, tied, and provided with a short button, which, being brought around the upright, is delicately held in position by a spear of dried grass or a delicate piece of wood." Jimmy baited his deadfalls with pinenuts impaled on the trigger. He had regularly set deadfalls for both small birds and animals in his younger days, and he still catches a few squirrels in this manner when he goes out pinenut gathering.

7
Four small sticks, two pinenuts,
a piece of string, and a flat rock—
with these the Indians built deadfalls which provided
the family with much of their meat.

8
Pinenuts are threaded on the trigger
to bait the trap.

9
Setting up the delicate trigger mechanism
required more than a little skill.

10
The trigger is set with tip-of-twig touching tip-of-twig.
At the slightest touch the whole structure will fall.

RABBIT PELTS, BUCKSKIN,
AND BARK

Little is known of the character of the clothing worn by the Indians of the Great Basin prior to the coming of the white man. Bits of description fell from the pens of the early travelers, but since most explorations took place in the summer months, there are few records of the manner in which the Indians protected themselves from the bitterly cold, dry winds that swept down the valleys and across the mountains in the winter, how they protected children from freezing, and how they tended for the new-born infant.

Rabbitskin blankets were vital to the life of every Paiute Indian. They were worn about the shoulders during the day and used as a blanket at night. They were soft and very warm, welcome even in the summer where desert nights are always cool. In winter they could mean the difference between life and death.

Hides from the larger animals, often assumed to be the primary source of clothing material for Indians, were difficult to obtain. Before the early settlers reduced the number of predatory animals, deer populations in the Great Basin were small, and kills by the Indians were infrequent. Antelope and mountain sheep, although more numerous, were the prize of only the most diligent hunter.

The method of using brains in tanning

was probably not different from that used in the Old Days. Paiute legend tells how greedy Coyote could not tan his deer skins because he foolishly ate the brains of the deer instead of saving them to soften the hides. Whenever skins were converted into clothing they were probably used without greatly altering their shape. Muskrat and beaver hides may have been sewed or tied together to make crude garments.

Moccasins made from buckskin were quite impractical in wet weather because they became soggy, and unless they were worn until dry, the leather hardened. Pacs and leggings of shredded sagebrush bark were occasionally used in the snow. Wuzzie said that badger skins, which are tough and greasy, were used untanned with the fur side in. She had also heard of a man who slipped his cold feet into a freshly skinned rabbit pelt.

In the summer the Indians usually wore little or no clothing. Men wore loin cloths—small patches of hide hung front and back from the ever-present thong that encircled their waists. The thong, probably the most necessary article of clothing for the hunter,

was used to carry rabbits and squirrels, as a weapon carrier for their rat sticks or an occasional arrow, or served as "pockets" for tools. Sandals made of rush were sometimes worn to protect feet from hot sand and sharp rocks.

Women usually wore some type of short skirt, leaving the upper part of their bodies bare except for strings of beads. Sagebrush bark and cattail leaves were woven into mats that were draped around shoulders or hung around the waist. Bowl-shaped baskets were used as hats without brims to protect the women's heads from the rub of the tumpline.

RABBITSKIN BLANKETS

Every year during the November drive, when the pelts were at their prime, hundreds of rabbitskins were taken and woven into blankets. Like the Old People, Jimmy George skinned his rabbits carefully to keep the entire pelt intact. He first cut the skin around the paws and then pulled it down the hind legs and off over the head.

1
For making rabbitskin blankets,
the rabbit is skinned with great care,
so that the pelt remains intact.

The knife he used was especially designed to be held in the teeth. The handle was of bone, flattened at the end for a secure grip. Sometimes he protected his teeth with a rag. Starting near an eye-hole, Jimmy cut the hide into a long, thin, spiral strip by pulling it up along the sharp edge of the knife. With skillful cutting Jimmy could make a fluffy ribbon ten to fifteen feet long from each hide. Then he formed a link in his chain of rabbitskins by tying the tip end of each fur ribbon through its own eye-hole.

2
Jimmy cuts the rabbit pelt
into one long strip as his grandfather did,
although his grandfather probably used
an obsidian knife.

3
To make a rabbitskin chain,
he formed links from the pelts
by tying the end of each skin
through its own eyehole.

Each giant fur link was looped through the last until he had a chain forty or more feet long. Tying one end to a tree he twisted the fur chain into a rope. In the Old Days the twisting was done by hooking the end of the chain onto a stick that was rolled along the thigh, much as cordage was made. In recent times, using a technique learned from watching white men make rope, the chain was tied to an off-balanced stick that was whirled. The skin side of the ribbon automatically folded in, leaving the soft fur

on the outside. Then the rabbitskin rope was hung up to dry, and afterwards the brittle ears were snapped off "because they become hard and scratch."

To weave a blanket the soft fur rope was looped around a crude loom of willows and twined together with strings of hemp or torn strips of rags. The desired coarseness of the weave was gauged by two, three, or four fingers held together. A man's blanket required a hundred rabbit skins, and a child's, forty.

4
Fastening one end of the chain to a tree,
Jimmy twisted it into a fur rope
by a rope-making method learned
from the white men.

5
The fur chain was tied to the short end
of an off-centered stick which was free
to rotate on the shaft Jimmy held
in his hand. When the stick
was whirled around the shaft,
the fur was twisted into a rope.

6
The dry rabbit ears
will be snapped off before the rope
is woven into a blanket.

TANNING HIDES

The art of tanning hides was re-learned by the Paiutes in recent years, but the process is undoubtedly similar to that used in the pre-white days. The modern tanning workshop consists of a cottonwood log about five feet long by seven or eight inches in diameter, from which the bark has been peeled. The log is dressed down to a satin finish with one end rounded off. It is leaned against a building with a protection of cloth or cardboard against the wall to keep the hide clean. In the Old Days the rib of a deer was used as a scraping tool, but now a dull draw-knife is preferred.

First the deer hide is soaked until the hair begins to slip. This may require a couple of days or a week, depending on the skin and the warmth of the weather. Formerly the Old People buried the hide in wet ground by the side of a stream. Today it is soaked in a bucket and the water is changed daily to control the unpleasant odor.

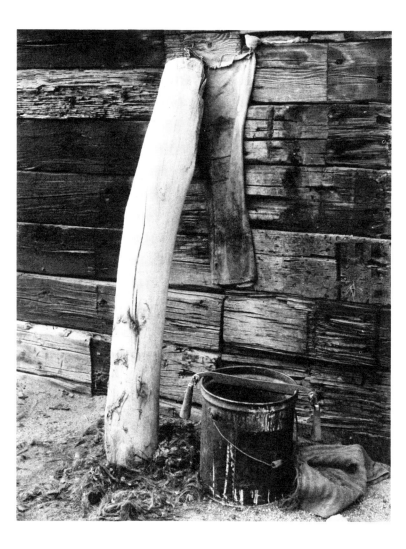

7
*In the modern tanning workshop,
a drawknife replaces the deer rib
used by the Old People.*

8
*Before scraping,
the hide is soaked in water
until the hair slips.*

Hanging the dripping hide over the end of the log, Johnny Dunn scraped off the hair which now slipped quite easily. The knife was drawn downward with firm pressure, taking with it the hair, and, if possible, the epidermis which lies under the hair. When wet, this membrane appears as a shiny surface on the white hide, but when dry it forms a hard, drawn area on the soft buckskin. Considerable skill is required to remove the epidermis completely without cutting the hide. If the skin became dry during the scraping process, it was sponged with handfuls of deer hair dipped in the buckets of water.

The hide was then ready for the tanning solution—made from brains and spinal cords. The brains were boiled, pressed through a sieve, and then returned to the broth. In the Old Days the brains of deer,

9
*Johnny was skillful
in scraping off the hair
without damaging the hide.*

10
*The hair is pulled out of the hide
rather than cut off.*

antelope, and even rabbit were used but now beef brains are preferred because they are more easily obtained. If extra brains were available, they were boiled and spread out to dry for use at a later date.

In this slurry of sieved brains, the hide was soaked over one night. By the following morning it was somewhat bleached and considerably swollen. It was then wrung out thoroughly and again placed over the post to be stretched and pulled continuously until completely dry. Every inch of the hide had to be worked, including the edges.

11
As in the Old Days, cooked brains still provide the chemical solution for tanning.

12
The scraped skin is allowed to soak in the brain slurry overnight.

13
Willy Jones stretched and kneaded the hide until it was completely dry.

To gain the golden tan color associated with buckskin, the Indians smoked the hide over a smoldering fire of willow chips. The modern method is to sew the tanned skin into the shape of a cylinder with a short skirt of denim attached to the bottom. A small fire built in a bucket is smothered with willow chips; the smoke rises through the hide cylinder as it would through a chimney. During the smoking process, the Indians keep close watch lest the chips burst into flame and consume both the hide and the shelter which protects it from the wind.

14
To obtain the proper shade of tan the hide must be watched carefully during the smoking process.

FIBER CLOTHING

Wuzzie made garments of shredded sagebrush bark that were probably authentic as to fabric but not pattern. She believes the Old People made sagebrush fiber mats that hung down in front and back with a hole in the center for the neck. They were tied on the sides, but had no sleeves.

First she pulled shaggy, loose bark in strips two or three feet long from the trunks of the head-high sagebrush growing in the river bottoms. Then she rubbed the bark between the knuckles of her clenched fists to soften it. Wuzzie wove a patch for a pair of sagebrush pants which she had previously made. Usually the fabric was made by twining the bark with cordage of hemp.

First she doubled the string, and into the loop she placed a small bundle of softened fibers. Then, after twisting the cord, she pressed another bundle against the first and twisted the cord again. More and more bundles were added and more and more rows of twine woven, until a rough fabric was formed. When the patch was finished, Wuzzie wove it into the pants.

81

15
*The longest bark fibers are found on the
large sagebrush which grows in the river bottoms.*

16
*To make a patch for a pair of sagebrush pants,
Wuzzie twines sagebrush bark with a piece of white cord.*

17
*When the patch was finished
Wuzzie wove it into the pants.*

The shirt she had made for Jimmy was similar to those which the Indians had copied from shirts worn by the early explorers. The pants were wrapped around the waist, and tied around the legs. Except for leggings and footgear, Wuzzie said, the men seldom wore sagebrush clothing in the Old Days.

The woman's blouse that Wuzzie made had sleeves. She said the Old People did not use sleeves and probably would not have opened the garment down the front. Wuzzie and Jimmy wear their sagebrush-bark clothing in parades and for exhibitions.

18
A man's sagebrush-bark shirt and pants . . .

20
A woman's blouse and skirt.

19
. . . with the pants stretched to full width, showing the buckskin ties for the legs.

21
The skirt probably resembles most closely the clothing worn before the time of the white man.

ARTICLES FROM SOFT FIBERS

Many small articles for comfort, household use, and play were made by the Paiute women from a large variety of plants. Usually the material could be gathered the year around as needed. Most of these items were for temporary use only and no great pains were taken with their manufacture.

During the time of plenty, when the marshes abounded with life, eggs of all kinds could be had for the taking. Ducks and geese were building down-lined nests on the shoreline, and mudhens were laying eggs in crude depressions on matted platforms of cattails. The Indians looked on this wealth of fresh eggs as a welcome change

from their winter diet. They knew where the redwinged blackbirds hung their nests on tule stems, defying trespassers, where yellowheaded blackbirds congregated in flocks that rose and fell like wind-blown leaves, defending their dominion with song, and they were not deceived by the pretended injuries of the fluttering killdeers.

To carry home the eggs, the women paused long enough to weave bags from tules that grew nearby. The bags had no set form of construction. The mesh was fine or coarse depending on the kind of food being gathered. The tule-bag was intended to be used only once. Men often made larger bags, Wuzzie said, a bushel or more in size to bring home their catch of fish or ducks.

It had been fifty years since Wuzzie as a child had made bags to gather eggs. Yet, when asked to show how it was done, her fingers never faltered.

In a marshy area where eggs were to be found, she waded knee-deep into the muddy water and pulled the long, uniform tules up by their roots. Then, sitting on the ground with her legs straight out in the manner of the Old People whose leg muscles had not been formed by years spent at a school desk, she began to weave the bag.[38]

TULE BAG

Choosing the longest tule for the weft, she flattened it between her thumbs and fingers. Twisting it once about the middle of a second tule stem, she kept adding more and more tules, twining the weft around each until the piece was as wide as she wished to make the bottom of the bag.

Then, bending the tules up so they formed the warp, she continued to twine the weft, spiralling it toward the top of the bag. When the tules became too short, she spliced them with others until the bag was as deep as desired. Often the bag was not finished beyond this point, so that the loose ends of the tules could be gripped at the top.

1
*After the base is formed,
the longer tules are bent up
to make the sides of the bag.*

2
*Wuzzie learned to make tule bags
from her grandmother in the Stillwater marshes
before the turn of the century.*

3
*Although the bags were usually made from tule,
sagebrush bark could also be used;
they varied greatly in size,
depending on the use
for which they were woven.*

Wuzzie showed how a handle could be added. She braided a few of the longest tules which projected from the top of the bag and tied them securely to the opposite side, splicing in new tules as needed. To finish the top she bent the tules over and bound them down snugly. The bag was flexible and strong and would hold three or four dozen eggs.

5
*With a new tule
she bound down the ragged ends
making a rim around
the top of the bag.*

4
*To make a handle,
she braided some of the
longest tules together.*

SPOONS

Wuzzie did not believe the Old People had spoons, but when her grandmother saw the spoons of the white people, she began making her own. She used the only technique she knew—weaving. She made spoons out of spikerush which, Wuzzie said, would last only a few days before drying out. When no longer usable, they were discarded and new ones made. Many Indians of the Great Basin had such spoons, and little girls even wove them in their play.

6
*The spikerush spoon,
casually discarded and easily replaced,
was used by the Old People to eat
the thick pinenut soup.*

7
*The bowl of the spoon was woven
and the handle was braided.*

8
*Spikerush was one of the many fibers used for making short-lived
objects—toys, shoes, and spoons. Wuzzie wove a toy
cradleboard such as she had played with when a child.*

A TOY CRADLEBOARD

The spikerush, a glossy stem that was tough either when wet or dry, was easily available and could be handled without preparation for many weaving purposes. Pliable and pleasant to the touch, it was made into sandals for wear on frozen ground, toy cradles for little girls, animal figures for the boys, and even spoons for eating the thick pinenut soup.

Wuzzie demonstrated how a toy cradleboard for a little girl could be woven of rush. These cradleboards did not last long, but they were easily replaced.

BRUSH OF GRASS ROOTS

Although some hairbrushes were made from the tails of porcupines, the most common were like those Edna Jones' mother regularly made for her family from the roots of the Great Basin wild rye grass. As girls, Edna and her sisters always used these brushes to groom each other's long, black hair.

These roots had to be collected in the winter months when the tall wild rye was

9
Edna Jones pulled the tough rootlets
from a clump of Great Basin wild rye grass
which had been soaked overnight.

10
She scraped the rootlets
to remove the soft outer covering
from the tough core.

dormant and each rootlet had become a tough cord covered with a spongy, fibrous coating. Then the Old Women searched out the most vigorous plants and loosened the stubborn root-clumps with their digging sticks.

From an overturned clump, which resembled a bristling hedgehog, Edna selected the long straight roots, and after she had soaked them for a few hours, she scraped them clean with a knife or a sharp stone.

11
A small bundle of roots
was then bound tightly
around the middle with hemp cord.

12
Edna bent the roots double . . .

13
. . . and tied them again.

Using fibers of hemp she tied a small bundle of roots together in the center. Then, folding them over, she made a second wrap around the bristles to bind the brush together, and trimmed off the uneven ends with scissors. In the Old Days the handle section would probably have been smeared with pitch.

Similar brushes were used as household tools to clean pinenut meal from the grinding rocks so that none would be wasted, and to remove ashes from the cooking rocks before they were dropped into the cooking baskets.

14
The brush was finished
by trimming the ends off evenly.

15
In the Old Days,
the hemp binding was pitched
to prevent slipping.

WILLOW WORK

The Paiute woman with her willow basket on her back was the burden bearer of the Indian community until about the middle of the 19th century when horses, and soon after, wagons, became common in the western part of the Great Basin. Since she carried not only the small children and the food but all the family's belongings as well, it was necessary that she keep her possessions at a minimum, her domestic objects lightweight and durable. Each woman needed one set of harvesting baskets; more were a burden. She made no pottery— pottery was heavy and easily broken. To survive the cold, each person in her family had a rabbitskin blanket. A second blanket was clumsy and unnecessary. The Paiutes felt there was no virtue in accumulating excess property. Even keeping the possessions of the dead came to be regarded as stealing, and the Indians believed that the ghosts would return to claim what was rightfully theirs.

At moving time, a woman packed the family possessions in a large basket on her back, which was suspended from her forehead by a broad tumpline. Only the heavy grinding stones were left behind. Into the large, coarse-woven conical basket, a wife first nested a fine-woven basket of the same shape. Into this she fitted a set of fine and coarse winnowing trays, the cooking basket, a looped willow stirring stick, and on top, the rabbitskin blankets. If she owned them, she took beads, an awl,[39] some fibers for cordage, red and white pigments for decoration and medicine, a bit of buckskin, a few herbs, and some food.

Most importantly, every woman carried bundles of long, slender willows which had been scraped white, and coils of willow sapwood that she had gathered and prepared during the winter months when the leaves were gone. These willows were the raw material necessary for the manufacture of nearly all of the family's household goods. From them she wove the tough little water jugs that she carried in her hand against thirst in the desert. From them she made cradles for the newborn infant, the hat that protected her head, the vessel in which she cooked, the bowl into which she served, and the tray on which she parched seeds, harvested berries, dried meats, cleaned nuts and roots, and with which she seined fish. From the willows she wove the beater with which she gleaned the seeds from the grasses, and the basket on which the seeds were collected. And finally, with these willows she made the basket in which she carried all the other baskets.

From the time the leaves fell in the autumn until the buds began to swell in the spring, the willows were ripe for gathering. Only the year-old wands without branches were chosen, and they were sorted as to size and length. The short, slender willows were saved for the hoods of cradleboards; long, coarser stems were laid aside for the warp of the burden baskets, water jugs, and winnowing trays, and the lattice work of the cradle. Those with the smallest leaf scars were split and peeled to obtain the tough, flexible sapwood—as necessary as thread to the seamstress—that was used for the weft in all basket weaving.

To prepare the weft, Wuzzie first scraped the buds from the willows. Then, gauging

1
The fine willow fiber used for the weft in basket making is the sapwood which lies between the bark and the heartwood. Wuzzie uses her teeth to start the splitting and to hold one side of the willow.

2
The willows are carefully split into three equal parts. Experience and skill are required to keep all parts the same thickness.

with her tongue and teeth, she split the willow lengthwise into three equal parts. As her fingers followed the split down the willow, she took care that all three sections remained the same size. When she had split the willow beyond her reach, she took a new grip with her teeth and continued splitting. Then she scraped the splinters from the pith with a knife.

3
When she has split
beyond her arms' reach,
she takes a new hold with her teeth
and continues splitting.

4
With a knife, she scrapes the splinters
from all three parts
at the same time.

5
To remove the sapwood,
she grips the heartwood in her teeth
and pulls the sapwood away from her.

To remove the sapwood, she cracked the pith about four inches from the end. Taking the woody center again in her teeth, and holding her fingers at the Y, she split the useless pith away leaving the sapwood and the bark. Returning to the other end of the willow, she removed the four-inch bit of pith that remained. The split willows were wound into a coil and stored for a few weeks until the bark dried and could be removed in a similar manner.

When dry, the bark peels from the sapwood quite easily. With the end of the sapwood in her left hand, Nina Dunn ran her index finger under the bark. She protected her finger from splinters by wrapping it

6
She slides her finger along the Y
to keep the two pieces from breaking.

7
This operation is repeated
from both ends of the stick
to insure a complete job. The sapwood
is then coiled with its bark
on for a couple of weeks
until slightly dry.

8
To remove the bark from the weft,
Nina holds the sapwood in her left hand
and runs her index finger
between the two.

with a bit of cloth. If the willow was of such quality that it did not break during this process, then the area from which it was gathered was worth revisiting. Before the willow weft could be used, it had to be dressed down, the loose fibers cut from the edges, and any unevenness trimmed off. In the Old Days this was done with the little crescent-shaped bits of obsidian frequently seen in old campsites. After the coming of the white man, the willows were scraped or drawn through a hole in a tin can.

Willows used for the warp were seldom split, but were scraped of their bark shortly after being gathered, and then were tied in bundles.

9
She covers her finger with a rag to protect it from splinters.

10
The long straight willows for the warp must be scraped clean of their bark while still fresh.

Although among the Paiutes there was little leisure time, bits of decoration were often added to the utility baskets. The prized red bark of the redbud tree which was common among the Washos in the Sierra mountains to the west was obtained only by trade, as were also the hanks of black bracken-fern root. Brown shades were obtained locally in two ways. Iron-bearing ore was ground into a powder and mixed in water with dried, ground plant material—clover or grass. Occasionally the sapwood was soaked in this iron-oxide solution until the proper shade of brown was achieved, after which it was woven into the basket. Sometimes though, this pigment was painted on the finished basket, using the frayed end of a stick as a brush. After it was dry, the residue was quickly rinsed away to avoid smearing.

It is difficult to find basket types which all the Paiutes agree are "true." Baskets showing the influence of neighboring groups in shape and design are in common use through trade and purchase, and are now accepted as their own.

11
Nina Dunn and Alice Vidovich
scrape the bark from a
winter's supply of warp.

12
Designs on basketry
are made by weaving in colored fibers.
Bracken-fern root is dyed by soaking it in a
rusty tin can or in a mixture of horse dung.

13
A hank of dyed bracken-fern root
ready to be split and trimmed
for weaving black designs,
and a coil of redbud weft,
with the bark left on,
for the red ornamentation.

CRADLEBOARDS

The arrival of babies was always welcomed by the entire Paiute family. Childless couples were pitied, and the old folks who had no grandchildren felt the lack keenly, since there was often a closer tie between grandparents and grandchildren than between parents and children. An orphan was not abandoned for there was sure to be an aunt, a cousin, or a grandmother who wanted him. A motherless baby was suckled by a relative, or kept alive by a patient old woman who dipped pinenut soup from the family bowl into its tiny mouth with her finger.[40]

When a baby was born, the mother rested about twenty-five days before resuming her duties, while the women of the family cared for both her and the baby. She kept warm, avoided meat, and bathed at intervals as prescribed by the custom of her own group.[41]

On the chance the baby might die, nothing was prepared in advance of its birth. As soon as the baby arrived, a grandmother or aunt made its first cradleboard. The first cradle, called a "boat-cradle," was usually made of unpeeled willows of rather crude workmanship, because it would soon be replaced. The newborn baby was wrapped in rabbitskins, dry algae, or matting of sagebrush rubbed soft, and was laced into the cradle with soft, buckskin thongs. The hood was said to mold the child's head. The mother carried the cradle under one arm, leaving the other hand free to do her work. As the baby grew, new cradles were made. When the child could hold up its head without support, it was placed in an elaborate buckskin-covered basket.

CRADLEBOARD FOR NEWBORN BABIES

With the basic materials for basket weaving—straight, peeled willows and coils of flexible sapwood—Nina Dunn made a boat-cradle which would hold a two-months-old baby easily. She wove the hood and the back in separate sections. The hood was then curved around and attached to the back, and the two sections were woven down the sides together. The willows were soaked to make them flexible, and strands from the coil of weft were kept in water until they were used.

As the weaving progressed, Nina shaped the sides and rounded hood. Later, small sticks were tied across the back for added support. The irregular ends at the bottom of the basket were trimmed off with a knife. In the Old Days they would probably have been broken off less evenly.

1
Nina Dunn made a cradleboard
for a newborn baby. The hood and back
were started separately, and then joined
together at the head. During the weaving process
the willow weft was kept moist
in a pan of water.

2
Cradleboards are made using the
characteristic Paiute twining technique.

3
During the weaving
the sides are shaped and the hood is rounded.

4
*As the baby grows,
larger cradleboards are frequently made.
This one held a two-months-old baby.*

5
*As a final step,
the foot of the cradleboard
is trimmed.*

Katy Frazier trimmed the lacing for the boat-cradle from long strips of the softest buckskin. Loops of buckskin were tied along both sides of the basket, and a long, thin thong was laced crisscross to keep the baby in place. Now babies are wrapped in blankets and placed on a quilted pad before lacing, but in the Old Days, basket linings were made from pelts of animals, or skins of ducks, geese, and swans.

In cold weather, infants were bundled in rabbitskin blankets with only their little brown faces showing. The swaddling provided security for restless, weeping babies who often fell asleep before the lacing was completed.

CRADLEBOARD FOR OLDER BABIES

The lovely design of the large cradleboard in use today, and for the past several generations, was probably borrowed from the Plains Indians and adapted to conditions in the desert. Archaeological evidence

6
*Katy Frazier trimmed a long, soft
buckskin thong for lacing the baby
into the cradleboard.*

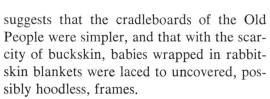

7
*She made buckskin loops
along each side . . .*

8
*. . . through which she passed
the crisscross lacing which held
the newborn infant in place.*

suggests that the cradleboards of the Old People were simpler, and that with the scarcity of buckskin, babies wrapped in rabbitskin blankets were laced to uncovered, possibly hoodless, frames.

The rim of the cradleboard was usually made of chokecherry branches, since they were less easily broken than willows. Long journeys to gather the chokecherry branches were made to the mountain streams where they grew.

A branch was bent around a form and allowed to dry. Edna Jones said the rim was less apt to break if the bark was left on while drying. Two chokecherry branches were needed for each cradle. They were lashed together at the sides with crossbraces tied between them. After the willow platform (which was woven in the same manner as the boat-cradle) was tied in place, the frame was covered with buckskin. Today, tan cotton fabric is sometimes substituted in cradles designed for summer use.

9
*For a larger cradleboard
a chokecherry frame is bent
around a form and dried.*

The hood, or sunshade, was woven from slender willows. Traditionally, diagonal lines of colored yarn across the top indicated a boy, while diamonds or zig-zag lines were for a girl. If the cradleboard was to be used for a second child, a new hood was always made, for the hood was considered

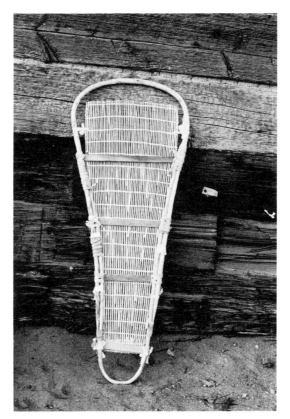

10
Two such chokecherry frames
are tied together for the head and foot,
and held in place with crossbraces.
A woven willow platform is added
for the baby to lie upon . . .

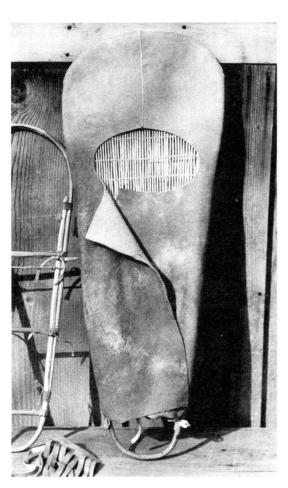

11
. . . and the frame is covered
with soft tan buckskin.

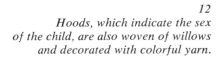

12
Hoods, which indicate the sex
of the child, are also woven of willows
and decorated with colorful yarn.

102

the personal property of the baby and great emphasis was placed on preserving it, no matter how badly battered.

A foot strap, often made from an old boot top, supported the child, and an old leather belt acted as a tumpline. Fine beadwork designs and buckskin fringe, usually threaded with large, colorful beads, were added for ornamentation only; they have no meaning. Occasionally the child's navel cord was placed in a tiny beaded pouch and added to the decoration. Sometimes trinkets, buttons, and loops of beads were hung from the hood as playthings.[42] An Indian baby loves his basket, feeling the security of being close to his mother while riding on her back or rocking on her knees.[43]

13
Katy applied a lovely beadwork design to the buckskin cover and then attached the hood from which she had hung beaded loops which were designed to entertain the child.

14
A heavy leather footstrap served to keep the baby from slipping out.

15
Katy completes the cradleboard by attaching the soft buckskin lacing.

BUILDING HOUSES

The Paiutes, dependent on hunting and gathering for survival, made shelters that were quickly and easily constructed. The Great Basin provided few sizeable animal hides for tepees, so for the Paiutes, shelters were at best only temporary structures made from grass, tules, cattails, sagebrush, willows, or pine boughs. When they needed shade for rest, they pulled brush up by the roots, leaned it against whatever was at hand, and crawled under. In their more permanent camps, the Indians wove slender willow withes into tight circular fences as protection from the wind that blew sand into eyes and food. For shade, they constructed shed roofs thatched with willows, called "willow shadows."

For protection from the cold in the mountain forests where fuel was abundant and logs were plentiful, large fires could be made, so only a minimum of shelter was needed. Semicircles of brush and branches, piled head high, broke the wind and reflected the warmth of the large logs burning in the center. Patched and repaired from year to year, abandoned when not needed, or burned when death occurred in them, shelters were mainly for protection from the elements. They were never "home."

The most complicated structure made by the Great Basin Indians was the willow-frame house covered either with mats of cattails or tules, or with long fringes woven of grass. When available, cattail leaves were preferred by the Old People because their flat surfaces shed moisture like shingles.

CATTAIL HOUSES

In April of 1958, Jimmy and Wuzzie George of Stillwater, Nevada, and Daisy Aster, Lily Shaw, and Dora John of Wadsworth, Nevada, made a small, temporary house of the size used as living quarters for one or two people, or for storage for food and implements, and occasionally for sweat houses.[44] Larger houses, more substantially built for families, would last five or more years, Wuzzie said. Everyone helped with the construction.

To build a house, Indian women required only a dozen long, strong willows to make the frame, large bundles of cattail leaves and willows for making mats, and willow withes, strings of sagebrush bark, or strips of old cloth to tie the building together.

Daisy and Dora dug small holes in the sand, loosening the ground with sticks and knives. Into these holes the willows were set and the dirt pushed in around them.

1
Dora John and Daisy Aster
"plant" a circle of willow poles.

Daisy and Jimmy tied circles of willows around the house to strengthen the uprights. An opening for a door was left in the lower row. The door always faced the rising sun, Lily said. In this case it was also away from the prevailing wind.

The second band of reinforcing willows drew the frame tighter, and formed the top of the doorway. When the third circle was added, the ends of the willows were pulled together abruptly to make the top of the house.

2
Using strips of cloth,
Daisy and Jimmy tie slender willows
around the uprights.

3
A second circle of willows
reinforces the frame and forms
the top of the door.

4
The third circle of willows
draws the frame together.

5
The top is left open
as a smoke hole.

6
*Three short willows form
the bottom layer of the cattail mat.*

With the framework finished, they began making cattail mats to cover the house. First they laid three slender willows on the ground, then spread an armload of cattails on them crosswise, and finally, placed three more willows on top. Ties were made through the cattails from the bottom to the top willows. Care was taken to include some of the cattails in the knots so that no holes were left for the wind to blow through. When the mat was finished, it was tied in place against the frame of the house.

7
*Jimmy and Daisy place the cattails
crosswise over the willows.*

8
*Three more willows hold
the cattail mat together.*

9
*The bottom and top willows
are tied together with strips of cloth
at intervals of a few inches.*

In this way, succeeding mats were made and fastened around the willow framework. The first row was placed at the bottom, and the second row overlapped on the outside for good drainage. Finally, a mat was made for the door. The only aperture left open in the finished house was a small smoke hole at the top.

Jimmy, Wuzzie, and Daisy had made many such houses before; Lily had lived in one but had never seen one made; Dora had heard of them, but had never seen one.

10
The cattail mat is lifted upright
and tied to the willow frame

11
More and more mats are made . . .

12
. . . and tied around the frame
until it is completely covered.
In successive years additional mats
are tied over weak places
in the walls.

13
Mabel Wright built frames
for a grass house and a sunshade.

GRASS HOUSE

Near Pyramid Lake in 1844, John C. Frémont noted that the Indians were living in houses of grass.[45] Mabel Wright made such a house 120 years later. She chose a site on a sandy bench where scattered chips of obsidian, broken manos and metates, and bits of charcoal testified that this had been a popular dwelling site for many generations. In fact, Mabel's great-grandparents had lived there in a grass house.

First Mabel gathered enough tall willows along the river for both the house and sunshade. As with the cattail house, the ends of the poles were buried in the sand and reinforced by circles of willows woven and tied in place.

Mabel had made the framework in the spring before the leaves were out, and she had to wait until the grass grew tall along the river bottoms before she could finish the covering. Like the Old People carrying their burdens of fuel and fiber—a familiar sight to the early settler in the Great Basin —she brought in loads of grass which she wove like hula skirts to cover the frame.

14
The frame is woven securely together
with long willows to withstand high winds.

15
Loads of grass are carried in
from the fertile river bottom
on the women's backs.

She hung row upon row of fringe on the framework and encircled them with willows to keep them from blowing away. The house, though only half finished, offered welcome shade. Piles of grass against the walls served as furniture for sitting and sleeping.

As the grass dried and became thin, Mabel made more and more fringes to cover the holes until a thick insulation was eventually formed.

16
Small bundles of grass
are twined together the way hula skirts are made.

17
Overlapping fringes of grass
are held down with willows . . .

18
. . . and grass is piled inside
for sitting and sleeping.

Mabel placed some of her treasures near the door: the rabbitskin blanket which she had woven, a conical burden basket, a fine-woven winnowing tray, a willow water jug, and a small individual serving bowl. Johnny Dunn's harpoon was there, and bits of jerky and dried cui-ui hung on racks demonstrated the manner in which food was stored long ago. Scraps of wood from the construction of the sunshade were laid for a fire.

In the winter, the shelter was warmed by a small fire burning in the center while the smoke curled up through the opening in the top. In the Old Days, as the first light showed in the east, smoke rose first from one and then more and more of the little grass houses until a haze hung over the little straw village. The Indians rose from their beds of grass and rabbitskins and stepped out of their doors to pray to the rising sun.

19
Mabel's grass house equipped in the Old Way.

Notes

[1] John C. Frémont, *Report of the Exploring Expedition to the Rocky Mountains in the year 1842, and to Oregon and North California in the years 1843-44,* 28 Cong., 2 sess., House Exec. Doc. 166 (1845) p. 219.

[2] For information on the Buenaventura River see John C. Frémont, *Narratives of Exploration and Adventure,* ed. Allan Nevins (New York: Longmans, Green & Co., 1956), footnotes pp. 372-373.

[3] I. C. Russell, *Geologic History of Lake Lahontan, a Quaternary Lake of Northwestern Nevada* (U.S. Geological Survey Monograph 11 [Washington, D.C.: Government Printing Office, 1885]), p. 288R; and Roger B. Morrison, *Lake Lahontan Stratigraphy and History in Carson Desert (Fallon) Area, Nevada* (U.S. Geological Survey Prof. Paper 424D [Washington, D.C.: Government Printing Office, 1961]), pp. D-111 to D-114.

[4] L. L. Loud and M. R. Harrington, *Lovelock Cave* ("Publications in American Archaeology and Ethnology," Vol. XXV, No. 1 [Berkeley: University of California Press, 1929]); and Robert F. Heizer and Alex D. Krieger, *The Archaeology of Humboldt Cave, Churchill County, Nevada* ("Publications in American Archaeology and Ethnology," Vol. XLVII, No. 1 [Berkeley: University of California Press, 1956]).

[5] The terms cattail and tule are often confused by individuals and in different regions. In this book cattail (Typha latifolia) refers to the flat-leaved marsh plant having a brown cylindrical seed-head. Tule (Scirpus acutus) refers to a tall round, pithy-stemmed rush which bears its seed-head near the tip of the stem.

[6] Frémont, p. 219.

[7] Explorers who speak of clothing include Frémont; Dan De Quille (William Wright), *Washoe Rambles* (Los Angeles: Westernlore Press, 1963), articles written in 1861; Captain J. H. Simpson, *Report of Explorations Across the Great Basin of Territory of Utah for a Direct Wagon-route from Camp Floyd to Genoa, in Carson Valley, in 1859* (Washington: Government Printing Office, 1876); and Edward M. Kern, "Journal of Mr. Edward M. Kern of an Exploration of Mary's or Humboldt River, Carson Lake, and Owens River and Lake in 1845," pp. 475-486 in Simpson's *Report.*

[8] Artifacts of antelope and mountain sheep outnumber those of deer in the archaeological sites in the Great Basin.

[9] Due to the fact that two or more sisters frequently married one man, the children of different mothers translate their relationship into English as sister-cousin or brother-cousin. The Paiute language does not distinguish between full sisters and sister-cousins. It does, however, distinguish between those siblings and cousins which are older or younger than they. The English term "cousin" is also extended to those who are distantly related and even to members of neighboring bands with whom blood ties exist.

[10] Sarah Winnemucca Hopkins describes very well the boy's puberty rites in her own band in *Life among the Piutes; Their Wrongs and Claims,* ed. Mrs. Horace Mann (Boston: G. P. Putnam's and Sons, 1883), pp. 50-51.

[11] Simpson, p. 106, gives a good description of husking the seed "which they separate from the husks by first rubbing the heads lightly under stones and then winnow, by throwing it up in the wind. Afterward they convert it into a flour by

rubbing it by hand between stones." De Quille, p. 53, also gives a description of gathering and grinding Indian rice grass.

[12] The use of sagebrush in conjunction with prayer is described by Wuzzie George as follows: "When your head not feel good, when you not feel good, talk to the sun and say, 'Help me!' We use sagebrush, put 'em in the water and shake 'em all over. Then just pray to the sun. Not take off clothes, just dressed like this, early in the morning—sometimes noontime too. Just any kind of water. Five days do that, and when you get through then stick sagebrush in the bush. Sagebrush dry up. Don't take [remove] it, just leave it there. Every morning my grandmother she always pray to the sun. I hear it. When the sun go down it put [carries] the sickness to the cold place. In the morning when sun come up, it [is] clean again and the sickness not show up no more. I guess that sun was [an] Indian long ago and he told everybody to pray."

[13] There seems to have been little tradition for protecting property from theft or for coping with those who learned to steal. "If a man had lost all of his food and was starving," I asked, "would it be all right for him to take somebody's pinenuts if he found them?" They did not know how to answer because, they said, a man would be ashamed to be in such a destitute situation.

Even today, whatever food is available is shared with the hungry guest or stranger. The standard greeting, which I have heard many times, is translated, "Have you eaten?"

If a meal is served while you are present, you are expected to eat without invitation. The food is not passed. You are expected to reach or ask for it. Meals are not served while unwelcome guests are present. Sensing this, they soon go away. Usually, only the incorrigibly lazy are considered unwelcome.

[14] Courting customs differed greatly not only between groups but between individuals within the group. One of the earliest written accounts of courting is in Sarah Winnemucca Hopkins' book, pp. 48–49.

[15] See also M. R. Harrington, "A Cat-tail Eater," *The Masterkey,* Vol. VII, No. 5. (September, 1933), pp. 147-149, a publication of the Southwest Museum, Highland Park, California.

[16] Small clusters of cooking rocks about the size of eggs can still be found in prehistoric camp sites. They are easily recognized because the frequent heating accelerated the weathering process.

[17] These woodpeckers were usually red-shafted flickers. However, lovely mobiles were also made from the wings of many other kinds of birds, including geese, ducks, and possibly magpies.

[18] One of my earliest recollections of the old Indian woman who ironed my ten little white dresses each week was hearing her tell this story about the flour and beans which her family had found when she was a child. It was not until I learned many years later the significance of the Indians' own powdery white pigment, that I realized why they had smeared the paste so disastrously on their rabbitskin blankets.

[19] Accounts of this battle may be found in Myron Angel, ed., *History of Nevada* (Berkeley: Howell-North Books, 1958), pp. 149–165 (a reproduction of the Thompson & West edition of 1881); and Sarah Winnemucca Hopkins, pp. 70–73.

[20] The first white people in Nevada often found it difficult to pronounce Indians' names and therefore encouraged the Indians to adopt such names as George, Sam, or Pete. George's son Jimmy would then, for instance, be called Jimmy George, and the name George would serve as the family's surname for each successive generation. Other Indians adopted an employer's family name, or were given a name by an Indian agent. Sometimes a white man would offer his own name to an Indian as a gesture of friendship.

To this day, Indians rarely use the titles of Mr. and Mrs. when speaking to each other; the main exception to this rule occurs in formal tribal meetings. Honorary titles such as captain (sometimes spelled capitan) were given by the Indians to men who were respected leaders. The title of rabbit-hunt captain or antelope-hunt captain was also occasionally given to men who had special ability in the hunt; their power was usually thought to be derived by means of magic.

Pronouns do not exist in the Paiute language, hence the confusion, when a Paiute speaks English, between "him," "her," "he," and so on.

[21] When I first saw the Doctor Rock (1952), it was little known to the white man. (It had been, however, referred to in reports as early as 1859 [Simpson, p. 87].) There were many very green pennies in the little holes pitting the top and sides of the rock. During the years that followed, I watched the offerings come and go. At one time there were safety pins, small white buttons, colored beads such as are used in bead-work, forty-two pennies, and even a small bit of black human hair. A few years later, the green pennies had disappeared. None have since been left long enough to corrode.

In 1954, I visited the rock with Alice Steve. She told me that the Indians prayed to the rock when they were going someplace. They asked "to feel good and to be happy." She said the rock was "good for wherever you sore. You pray and the rock give it [health] to you." She demonstrated by half reclining over the rock and bringing her right leg up partly over it. At the same time she prayed, lifting her head slightly. She spoke aloud in Paiute and told me later that she had prayed for the soreness to go out of her leg. It is very important that when something is asked, a payment be made. The rock is considered to own these payments, so it is stealing to remove them. "Those beads belong to that rock. You pay him that, so it belong to him," Wuzzie said. "Sometime we stop there when we go to Schurz to gamble. We ask to win. We give paint or beads. Beads best. I guess long time ago, Indians make beads from duck bone. When sick, give Doctor Rock those beads. Now money's the best pay. Coyote make that writing [petroglyphs] on rock."

The last time I made a visit, however, there were no pennies on the Doctor Rock. A highway construction crew had bulldozed it out of the right-of-way.

[22] Deer-hoof rattles were made by soaking the hooves until the outer cone-shaped shell could be struck off with a stick. Jimmy drilled a hole in the top of each cone and hung it on a buckskin thong. Clusters of the shells were tied thus on a short handle. The rattles were used for both doctoring and dancing.

[23] A buckskin rattle was made out of the untanned skin of a deer's ear from which the hair had been scraped. The wet hide was molded and tied around a hard ball of mud and allowed to dry. Then the mud ball was broken and the dirt shaken out. The handle goes completely through the rattle with the tip extending out the top. In modern times a discarded electric light bulb is often used as a mold instead of a mud ball, and the glass shattered for removal.

When the rattle was to be used for dancing, it was filled with the small, well-sorted gravel found in the big anthills of the mountains. Those rattles to be used for doctoring contained special beads. Beads were believed to have healing power. For instance, if an Indian had a headache, possibly caused by a whirlwind, a doctor would dream about a certain color bead and prescribe that it be tied onto a strand of the patient's hair for a few days. Then the bead was buried in moist dirt beside a running stream where the water could wash away the headache (or cool a fever). Rattles such as this may be a recent addition to the Paiute culture.

[24] Pyramid Lake has dropped ninety feet since the coming of the white man. This has been due to the increased use of water in the Truckee Meadows, where Reno is situated, and the diversion of water into the Lahontan Reservoir for the first U.S. Reclamation Project.

[25] This story is also told very vividly by Sarah Winnemucca Hopkins, pp. 41–43.

[26] Hogs that had escaped from early ranchers multiplied so fast in the marshes of Carson Sink and Carson Lake that by 1890, the cattlemen decided to round them up and sell them to the mining camps. With the aid of horses and dogs, many hundreds were caught in the drives. Their eyes were sewn shut to keep them from scattering and they were herded across the desert. According to Jack Sheehan, who accompanied the drive, five hundred went to Virginia City, two hundred and fifty to Bodie, two hundred to Bellville, and so on.

[27] The Indians gathered a type of sugar from the common reed (Phragmites communis), somewhat resembling a slender cornstalk, which grows near springs and on river banks. In the summer it is attacked by myriads of aphids. At the point where the aphids puncture the underside of the leaf a small drop of honeydew forms. If a rain has not washed the drops away, the Indian women cut and stack the plants in the fall. When dry, the stalks are held over a fine-woven tray and the dried honeydew beaten off. This was virtually the only sweet the Paiutes knew, since honey-gathering bees are not native to North America.

[28] Jack Wilson was called Wovoka by James Mooney in "The Ghost-dance Religion and the Sioux Outbreak of 1890," *Fourteenth Annual Report of the Bureau of Ethnology to the Secretary of the Smithsonian Institution, 1892–93* (Washington, D.C.: Government Printing Office, 1896). Today, however, the only Indians who recognize him by that name are those who have read the report.

[29] Pinenuts require two years to mature. Wuzzie said that when the Indians were gathering pinenuts in the fall, they watched for the little cones that would be the next year's crop. When they found some immature pinenuts they put a small pine bough bearing the cones into a mountain spring. Sagebrush was placed over the bough, "because sagebrush is a medicine," and weighed down with a rock. Wuzzie said, "We talk to it and say, 'Don't get dry. We are going to eat you next fall.' "

[30] Simpson, p. 85; and Kern, p. 480.

[31] Captain Wasson, a Paiute from Schurz, made exquisite rabbit nets. When he died, ca. 1904, the net was cut in half. One half was given to each daughter, Mary and Sally. The portion given to Mary was lost. The other half was put away and saved. Later, Sally had planned to burn it, but Ida McMasters, her daughter, said to keep it. When it was displayed at the community fair in the church at Schurz, Miss Alida C. Bowler paid $300 for it. Miss Bowler was Superintendent of the Carson Indian Agency during the late 1930's. This net is probably the one on display at the Wa-Pai-Shone Trading Post at Schurz, Nevada.

Edna Jones remembers her grandfather, Captain Wasson, sitting naked in the sun to make string for his nets. He always wore his hair long with a sweatband tied around his head. As he stripped the hemp fibers, he laid them out lengthwise in front of him, and tied them at one end so they could be pulled out as needed to make string. As the string was finished, he wound it on a board twelve to fourteen inches long, notched at the ends.

A greasewood stick thrust in the ground held the net upright during the drive. It was notched in such a way that it would release the net upon impact, letting it fall to entangle the rabbit. Captain Wasson would transport his net by horseback to a place where he would meet the other groups of drivers who also had nets. The nets were then stretched end to end, across the desert. All the rabbits caught in his net belonged to him.

After a snowstorm, the whole immediate family of Sing McMasters would have a rabbit drive. Since the family consisted of two wives (daughters of Captain Wasson) and nine children, they were able to net many rabbits. (Personal communication with Edna Jones.)

[32] Hunters frequently used sticks which they would thrust into animal holes. If the stick struck home, the hunter would twist it into the fur so as to pull the rodent from

the hole. Hunters also impaled rodents when they attempted to bite the stick.

Rat is an inclusive term used by the Paiutes for many small rodents such as kangaroo rats, mice, muskrats, gophers, ground squirrels, and chipmunks.

The most desirable husband was the man who came home at night with a dozen or more rats hanging from the thong around his waist.

[33] Early-day pitfalls are described in O. B. Huntington, *Eventful Narratives* ("Faith Promoting Series" [Salt Lake City: Juvenile Instructor Office, 1887]), pp. 77–98.

[34] Blinds of brush and stone behind which a hunter could conceal himself were built in passes and near springs. The stone blinds are still plainly visible in many parts of the Great Basin.

Wuzzie's father made blinds for duck hunting. Wuzzie said that the wind lived in holes in the southwest part of the valley and that when the whirlwinds came out of the holes, the wind would blow. Wuzzie's father watched for the whirlwinds because he knew that when the wind blew, the ducks would become restless and fly from pond to pond. For a blind he made a round house out of brush between the lakes and shot the ducks when they flew over.

"On warm, sunny days," Wuzzie said, "ducks just sit in one place and be lazy, like people." I asked Wuzzie if her father's gun had just one shell. "No," she said. "No shells. Just pour powder down barrel and put in anything and push [it] down with stick."

[35] The Indians believed that Porcupine made the storms—snowstorms in particular. When a hunter killed a porcupine, he carefully buried its entrails lest a storm overtake the family.

[36] The antelope hunt is graphically described in Hopkins, pp. 55–57.

[37] Simpson, p. 53.

[38] While interviewing the Indians, I was struck by the fact that those women who could sit on the ground for long periods of time with their legs straight out often knew the most about the Old Ways. On inquiring, I found that these people had been schooled by their grandparents rather than at the desks of the white man.

[39] Awls were usually slender fragments of polished bone, but Wuzzie said they also used the bill of a "hell-diver," or grebe.

[40] Jimmie George's mother died when he was "still in his basket." His grandmother fed him in this manner. (Personal communication with Wuzzie George.)

[41] A good description of birth customs is given by Sarah Winnemucca Hopkins, pp. 49–50. The following are three methods of birth control related to me by the Indians: burial of a stillborn child face down; burial of the placenta in a hole where it will be eaten by gophers; drinking of a tea brewed from dodder, a parasitic plant.

[42] If a baby in a basket played with a set of twins, a bead from his basket had to be given to each of the twins lest the child one day become the parent of twins himself.

[43] The cradleboard is an ideal way for carrying children in the desert and mountains. I personally used a cradleboard to carry each of my children, and they were delighted with it. The modern mother is beginning to discover its successors—the plastic baby tote and the pack-board.

[44] Wuzzie's account of a sweathouse: "Sam Dick made a small sweathouse for two people. He make a fire outside and put rocks in fire. When rocks hot he take inside. Have cold water in house to put on the rocks to make steam. Then Indian rub themselves with their hands, not use rag. Put clothes on when they go outside. Women take baths too. Sometimes the sweatbath is used when people don't feel good. Put straw on the floor. Use for rheumatism and colds. They pray to the sun. Sometimes men, sometimes men and women, sometimes just women use house."

[45] Frémont, p. 218.

Glossary

Canada goose	nagíta
carved seed	kammísɨkɨ
Cattail-eaters	tóidɨkaʔa
Cui-ui-eaters	kuyúidɨkaʔa
desert thorn	húupui
great horned owl	muhú
ground squirrel	kɨbí
Ground-squirrel-eaters	kɨbídɨkaʔa
hemp	wɨhá
Jackrabbit-eaters	kammídɨkaʔa
mentzalia seed	kuhá
mosquito	mopoŋɨ
mustard seed	atsá
nutgrass	áabi
the people's bones (graveyard)	nɨmíʔohó
the People's Father	nɨmínnaa
rice grass	wái
salmon trout	agai
spring trout	tamáʔagai
Sucker-eaters	pakwídɨkaʔa
Trout-eaters	agáidɨkaʔa
white man	táiboʔo
willow skin (bark)	sɨ̈bi puá
winter trout	tommóʔagai

The following symbols are used in spelling out Northern Paiute words: /ɨ/ for the vowel sound in American English *just* when occurring, for example, in the sentence *he just left;* /ŋ/ for the nasal sound in English *sing;* /ʔ/ for the glottal catch as, for example, the initial sound often heard in the emphatic exclamation *ouch!* A long vowel is written as two identical short vowels, as in *húupui* 'desert thorn.'

Offset by SPO, Carson City, 1968